Free to Be Me with a BFRB

of related interest

The BFRB Recovery Workbook
Effective Recovery from Hair Pulling, Skin Picking, Nail Biting and Other Body-Focused Repetitive Behaviors
Dr. Marla Deibler and Dr. Renae Reinardy
ISBN 978 1 83997 655 1
eISBN 978 1 83997 656 8

The BFRB Workbook for Teens and Young Adults
Recover from Skin Picking, Hair Pulling, and Other Body-Focused Repetitive Behaviors
Dr. Laura Chackes with Lauren McKeaney
ISBN 978 1 80501 865 0
eISBN 978 1 80501 866 7

Crushing OCD Workbook for Kids
50 Fun Activities to Overcome OCD with CBT and Exposures
Natasha Daniels
Illustrated by Richy K. Chandler
ISBN 978 1 83997 888 3
eISBN 978 1 83997 889 0

ADHD Is Our Superpower
The Amazing Talents and Skills of Children with ADHD
Soli Lazarus
Illustrated by Adriana Camargo
ISBN 978 1 78775 730 1
eISBN 978 1 78775 731 8

FREE TO BE ME WITH A BFRB

The Ultimate Kids' Guide to Living Well with Hair Pulling, Skin Picking, Nail Biting, and Other Body-Focused Repetitive Behaviors

Dr. Jennifer Gola, Dr. Marla Deibler, and Dr. Renae Reinardy

Illustrated by **Rebecca Price**

Jessica Kingsley Publishers
London and Philadelphia

First published in Great Britain in 2026 by Jessica Kingsley Publishers
An imprint of John Murray Press

1

Please be aware this book contains depictions of bullying, big feelings, and BFRB-associated behaviors.

A CIP catalogue record for this title is available from the British Library and the Library of Congress

ISBN 978 1 80501 905 3
eISBN 978 1 80501 906 0

Printed and bound in Great Britain by Bell & Bain Limited

Jessica Kingsley Publishers' policy is to use papers that are natural, renewable, and recyclable products and made from wood grown in sustainable forests. The logging and manufacturing processes are expected to conform to the environmental regulations of the country of origin.

Jessica Kingsley Publishers
Carmelite House
50 Victoria Embankment
London EC4Y 0DZ

www.jkp.com

John Murray Press
Part of Hodder & Stoughton Ltd
An Hachette Company

The authorized representative in the EEA is Hachette Ireland,
8 Castlecourt Centre, Dublin 15, D15 XTP3, Ireland (email: info@hbgi.ie)

To every kid with a BFRB—

This book is for you.

For the moments when it feels like no one else understands.

For the times you've tried so hard to stop and still kept going.

For the questions you've had but were afraid to ask.

You are not alone.

You are brave, curious, creative, and strong.

You are more than your BFRB—and you always have been.

May these pages remind you of your strength,

introduce you to friends who've walked a similar path,

and help you discover all the tools already inside of you.

You are worthy of kindness, patience, and hope.

Exactly as you are.

With love and belief in you,

Drs. Gola, Deibler, and Reinardy

Contents

Special Acknowledgments

This book would not be what it is without the incredible individuals who so generously and courageously shared their "Just Like Me" stories with us—and with you. To Christy Garner, DC, Michael Herold, Aneela Idnani, Clare Mackay, PhD, Lauren McKeaney, Gessie Perez, and Doug Schwarz: thank you from the bottom of our hearts.

Your openness, strength, and honesty have lit a path for young readers navigating their own journeys with body-focused repetitive behaviors (BFRBs). Because of your voices, children will feel less alone, more understood, and more hopeful. You've helped show that living with a BFRB is only one part of a vibrant, successful, and meaningful life.

Your bravery in being seen, your compassion in being heard, and your commitment to making the world a better place for the next generation is nothing short of inspiring. Thank you for being fierce advocates and living proof that healing and thriving are possible.

This book is for the kids—and it's also for the heroes like you who make sure they know they are never alone.

All pages marked with ✦ can be downloaded at http://jkp.com/catalogue/book/9781805019053

What's This All About? An Introduction for Parents, Professionals, and Kids

LETTER TO PARENTS AND PROFESSIONALS (A SPECIAL LETTER TO KIDS WILL FOLLOW THIS):

Hello, and welcome.

As psychologists specializing in body-focused repetitive behaviors (BFRBs), OCD, and related conditions, we understand the challenges that come with supporting a child struggling with a BFRB. Dr. Deibler and Dr. Reinardy previously co-authored *The BFRB Recovery Workbook*, a resource for older teens, adults, and professionals treating BFRBs. You may find it to be a valuable companion as you expand your understanding of these conditions and the strategies used to manage them.

This workbook is designed for children ages 7 to 12, helping them develop a new relationship with their BFRB through curiosity, self-compassion, and effective coping skills. Through engaging activities, kids will learn to identify triggers and develop healthier coping skills.

While we introduce many effective strategies, not all need to be practiced, and most children will benefit from adult support.

Take your time—one to three new skills per week allows for

meaningful progress. A gradual approach encourages self-care, builds confidence, and fosters realistic, long-term management of the child's BFRB. If you and your child need a slower pace, that's fine, too. Our goal for you is to set your own pace based on your individual needs and level of comfort in using and practicing the relevant skills. We encourage prioritizing curiosity and fun in working through this material above all else. This shouldn't be a chore, but rather, we hope it's an adventure in self-discovery and skill building to help kids thrive in who they are and in whatever they choose to do.

As caregivers and professionals, we know how hard it is to see a child struggle. As mothers, we also understand the emotional weight of wanting to help. Please know that if you are here as a parent, your child's BFRB is not your fault, and your support is invaluable. BFRBs are more than habits and cannot simply be willed away. By seeking resources like this workbook, you are taking an important step in guiding your child with patience and understanding.

At the same time, remember that this is *their* journey. Your child is so much more than their BFRB. Encouragement, skill-building, and celebrating effort will be far more effective than punishment or shame. Positive reinforcement fosters resilience, while over-focusing on the behavior itself can backfire, resulting in an increase in the behavior, lack of progress, and/or interpersonal conflict.

Caregivers and therapists may benefit from their own support networks, whether through support groups, professional training, or collaboration with pediatricians and dermatologists. There are community resources available. If you struggle to find those supports, please feel free to reach out to us directly; we'll happily provide specific recommendations. Also, note that not all children will be ready to work on their BFRB right away, and that's okay—what matters most is letting them know help is available when they are ready. We encourage you to let them lead.

This workbook includes "Just Like Me" stories—real accounts from individuals who grew up with BFRBs. These stories remind children that they are not alone and that they can lead fulfilling lives, no matter the condition of their hair, skin, or nails. Recovery looks different for everyone, but our goal is to help the child in your life develop self-compassion, build meaningful skills, and focus on what truly matters.

Thank you for taking this important step in supporting your child.

Warmly,

Dr. Jennifer Gola, Dr. Marla Deibler, and Dr. Renae Reinardy

LETTER TO KIDS:

Welcome to your workbook!

We are experts in body-focused repetitive behaviors (BFRBs) like skin picking, hair pulling, or nail biting. In this book we would like to share what we have learned from working with amazing kids like you for over 25 years!!

First, you should know this: **you are not alone**. That's why we've included real stories from happy, successful grown-ups who were kids just like you. We've called these "Just Like Me" stories to help you to meet real people who have had a similar journey. You'll also meet our book characters, Maya and Elliot, who will help guide you through some of the skills and tools you'll learn.

In this book you'll find tons of cool things to learn about yourself and your BFRB. As you turn the pages, you'll discover skills to help you *ride the waves* of big emotions, spend more time enjoying life, and feel more in control of your thoughts and behaviors.

You'll also learn why your BFRB might be showing up, and gain awesome life skills to help you say "Thanks, but no thanks!" to those BFRB urges.

Some parts of the book you can do on your own, while others are great to go through with a parent, therapist, or another special adult in your life.

And remember—this isn't a race! Work on this at your own pace. You don't need to finish the book in one day or even one week. We suggest working through at least one section of a chapter at a time, up to one chapter at a time at the most. Try practicing one to three skills that you learn each week. We hope that you'll find it interesting and sometimes even fun to learn about yourself and your BFRB. Just like learning to ride a bike, it takes time, patience, and practice. You might wobble at first, but the more you practice, the easier it gets—and before you know it, you'll have new, healthy habits that make you feel great.

We're so excited for you to start this journey, and we're cheering you on every step of the way!

Dr. Jennifer Gola, Dr. Marla Deibler, and Dr. Renae Reinardy

Part 1

GET READY

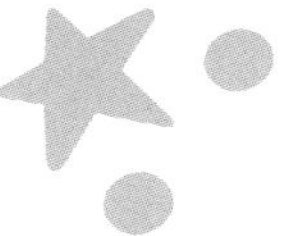

Chapter 1

All About Body-Focused Repetitive Behaviors (BFRBs)

"Just Like Me"

By Lauren McKeaney, Founder of Picking Me Foundation

My name is Lauren, and I used to really hate the color red. And polka dots. Especially red polka dots.

You see, when I was younger, I did something every day that I didn't want people to know. I picked my skin. It wasn't something I meant to do, but I just couldn't help it. Sometimes, it was because my skin would itch, or I had a bug bite or a scrape or bump, and I would just keep picking at it. Afterward, I would feel really bad, but I still couldn't stop. My mom and dad would get upset and tell me to stop, but it was hard to explain that I couldn't stop.

I didn't like wearing red or polka dots because they reminded me of the picked red spots on my skin that I didn't want people to see. I would try to hide them, but when I wore red or polka dots, it felt like everyone would notice my picked skin more. So, I decided to never, ever wear them.

Growing up skin picking all the time was hard and lonely. Every time I picked, I felt bad about myself. And even though I smiled a lot and looked happy, I was really struggling and embarrassed inside. Sometimes I would get blood on my clothes and try to hide it so my mom wouldn't see. I didn't want to go to sleepovers with my friends because I was afraid I would pick my skin and bleed on their sheets. I didn't know how to tell doctors that I wanted to stop picking but couldn't. And I thought I was the only one in the world who did this.

But then, I found out I wasn't alone! There are actually many people who have something called BFRBs (body-focused repetitive behaviors) like skin picking, just like me! Learning that other people felt like I did made me feel a lot better. As I felt better, I learned how to manage my skin picking and not pick as much.

The less I picked, the more I wanted to help others do the same too. So, I started a nonprofit called the *Picking Me Foundation* to help people understand skin picking, give them hope, and help them heal.

Now, as the President of *Picking Me*, I get to do something that makes me happy every day. I help parents understand what their kids are going through, teach doctors how to help, and support people who are trying to stop picking. And guess what? I even made the symbol for my company red polka dots, and now, every time I see them, I smile!

Oh, and I love wearing red now too! :)

Lauren

Lauren is brave to have shared her journey with skin picking—her BFRB. You may have some of the same thoughts and feelings about your BFRB as she did.

We are going to explore your journey with a BFRB. But first, let's back up to the basics!

SO, WHAT IN THE WORLD IS A BFRB?

BFRB stands for **body-focused repetitive behavior**, but that's a mouthful—so we just say **BFRBs**! A BFRB is when someone pulls their hair, picks their skin, bites their nails or the inside of their cheeks, picks their nose, or does any other kind of biting, chewing, pulling, or picking of their hair, skin, or nails.

But, don't many kids pick their nose, pick at their scabs, or pull at that hair that is out of place?

Yes! This is all very normal. Adults and kids groom themselves. And even animals lick and nibble at their fur or pull at their feathers.

A behavior is called a BFRB when you try to stop or do it less often, but it feels really hard to stop! It can also be a BFRB if it's making things hard for you—for example:

- if you feel like you need to wear a hat to hide a bald spot so that others don't find out
- if you spend so much time picking your skin that you miss out on fun
- if your skin gets sore or infected.

Some people call this a "habit" because it's something you do over and over, sometimes without even realizing it. But when that habit starts causing problems or making you feel upset, that's when it's called a BFRB.

WHICH BFRB(S) DO YOU HAVE?

Here is a list of common BFRBs and their long medical terms (see if you can pronounce them!). Circle the behaviors you have some trouble with.

- ✓ Hair Pulling (Trichotillomania)
- ✓ Skin Picking (Excoriation Disorder)
- ✓ Nail Biting (Onychophagia)
- ✓ Nail Picking (Onychotillomania)
- ✓ Nose Picking (Rhinotillexomania)
- ✓ Cheek Biting (Morsicato Buccarum)
- ✓ Lip or Tongue Biting (Morsicatio Labiorum or Morsicatio Linguarum)
- ✓ Hair or Skin Eating (Trichophagia or Dermatophagia)

A lot of kids with a BFRB think they're the only ones who have it. But guess what? You're not alone—not even close! We wouldn't write this book if only a few kids had BFRBs. In fact, MILLIONS of kids, teenagers, and even adults have them too! There are probably other kids at your school who have a BFRB—you just might not know because some people hide it, or it's not easy to see.

The most common BFRBs are hair pulling, skin picking, and nail biting. People who pull their hair might pull from anywhere hair grows, like their scalp, eyelashes, eyebrows, arms, legs, or even underarms. People who pick their skin might pick from different places, like their scalp, face, arms, legs, or stomach. And nail biting? Some bite their fingernails—and even their toenails too!

If you pull your hair, pick your skin, or bite your nails, circle or color in where you pick, pull, or bite on your body!

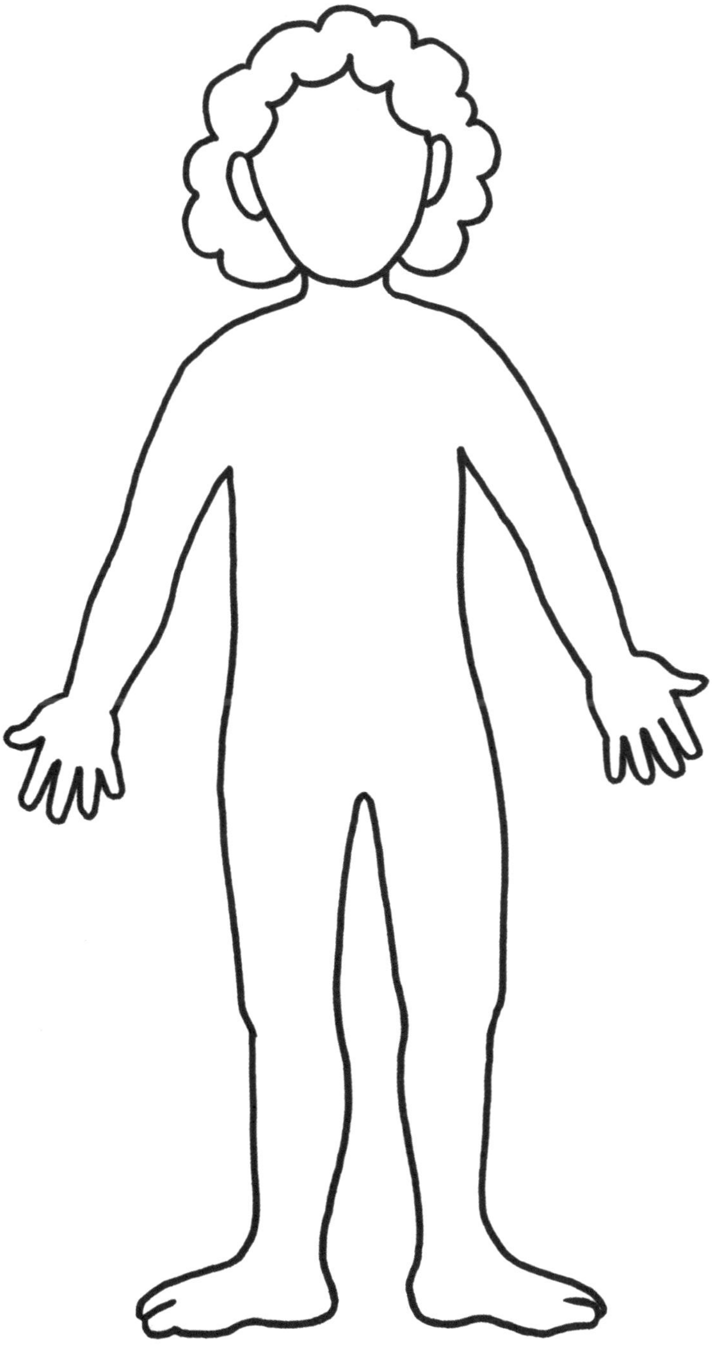

WHY DO I HAVE A BFRB?

If you're wondering why you have a BFRB, that's a great question! Scientists aren't completely sure what causes BFRBs, but we do know they can run in families. Just like you are passed down genes by your parents which mean you might have the same eye color, hair color, or freckles as your parents or grandparents, the urge to pick, pull, or bite can be passed down through genes too.

Also, everyone's brains and bodies work a little differently! Just like some kids love chocolate ice cream while others prefer strawberry or mint chocolate chip, some kids feel the urge to pull their hair, pick their skin, or bite their nails, while others don't. Though they might instead have big fears or worries, or have trouble staying still and focusing, or another type of difficulty. It's just part of what makes each person unique!

What are some things about you which have been passed down through your family's genes? Ask a family member if you are unsure!

....

....

....

....

....

What is your favorite ice cream flavor? And, what are your favorite things to do for fun?

....

....

....

....

....

Ask three other people these questions and see if they have different answers from you! Write each person's name and answers below!

....

....

....

....

....

Why do you think they might have different answers?

....

....

....

....

....

Even though we don't know exactly what causes BFRBs, we do know why they can be hard to stop. Kids do BFRBs for lots of different reasons.

Many kids like the way it feels—it might feel good on their skin, scalp, or in their mouth. Some like the feeling of making rough skin smooth or chewing on a nail. If it didn't feel good in some way, you probably wouldn't do it!

BFRBs can also help kids feel calmer, give them something to do when they're bored, or even help them focus.

Lots of kids pick, pull, or bite when they feel anxious or worried.

We're here to help you figure out some of the reasons you do your BFRB later in this book!

Think about what you like about doing your BFRB. How does it help you? Does it make you feel calm, help you focus, or get rid of feelings you don't like? Write down the ways your BFRB makes you feel better.

How does my BFRB help me feel better?

How does my BFRB help me get rid of thoughts, feelings, or sensations in my body that I don't like?

People feel all kinds of emotions about their BFRB, and that's okay! Some kids feel embarrassed or ashamed, especially if a parent has told them to stop—over and over again—or if they've been teased about it. That can make kids feel sad, angry, or frustrated. And sometimes, feeling sad or embarrassed can make kids want to pick, pull, or bite even more—it's a tricky loop!

This space is for you to write or draw thoughts about your BFRB. You might have a lot of thoughts while reading this book, like:

Maybe you are having thoughts like these or maybe you are noticing other thoughts. What thoughts are you having as you read this?

All of those thoughts are okay! Instead of judging them, try to just notice them—like a curious puppy sniffing around a new neighborhood.

Some kids want to stop their BFRB but have a hard time, while others don't want to stop at all. A lot of kids feel **both** ways—they might want to stop for some reasons but also want to keep doing it for others. And guess what? That's totally okay!

Let's take a closer look at your BFRB journey. Try to be **curious** about it, like a detective setting out to solve a mystery. Remember, there are no right or wrong answers. Just be honest with yourself—this is all about learning more about *you*.

Do you remember when you first started doing your BFRB? If so, write about it here: How has your BFRB made you feel about yourself?

....

....

....

....

....

Does your BFRB take up a lot of your time?

....

....

....

....

....

Does your BFRB cause any damage to your body or to your health?

....

....

....

....

....

Do you hide your BFRB from other people? If so, who do you hide your BFRB from?

....

....

....

....

How do the grown-ups in your life talk about your BFRB? How do you feel when they talk about it?

....

....

....

....

Write some reasons why you might want to keep your BFRB just the way it is. What do you like about it? How does it help you?

....

....

....

....

Write some reasons why you might want to work on changing your BFRB. How could things be better for you? What would you like to be different?

....

....

....

....

....

....

What do you hope to learn from this workbook?

....

....

....

....

....

....

....

....

....

....

Draw a picture of yourself in this space, with your BFRB.

Now that you've finished your drawing, take a moment to look at it. How does the drawing make you feel? Is this different from how you want to look or feel?

....

....

....

....

How do you want to look or feel? Go ahead and draw yourself as the "you" who you most want to be.

Now, let's make it happen!

Chapter 2

This Is Me (and My BFRB)

"Just Like Me"

By Aneela Idnani, HabitAware and BFRB Changemakers Nonprofit Founder

My little mind created big problems for me. As a child I struggled to fit in—I was growing up as an Indian American, with parents who moved to the US from India, and also as a "tomboy" who didn't feel girly like the other girls. And, on top of that, my father got cancer when I was a teenager. I felt overwhelmed and sad. I had a lot of negative thoughts. This is when I started to pull out my hair.

I started pulling the hair from my private area first as a tween and then started pulling my eyebrows and eyelashes. Although it felt good when I was doing it, I thought it was weird—and that *I* was weird and ugly for doing it.

I told myself that friends wouldn't like me and I'd never find love. So, I hid because I was afraid people would think bad thoughts about me and I felt embarrassed and ashamed. In my late 30s when I was pregnant with one of my children, I noticed my hair pulling got worse and my husband noticed. When my husband gently asked

"Aneela, where are your eyebrows?" I shared my hair pulling secret. By this time, I had learned that this was called trichotillomania, but that label only made me feel more shame and embarrassment and I tried to cover up my missing eyebrows and eyelashes with makeup.

With my loving husband by my side, we set out to change my sad trichotillomania story. We invented a smart bracelet that helps people become more aware of their BFRB by providing a gentle vibration when their hand is positioned to pick, pull, or bite—I thought that if I am aware that I'm pulling, I can do something about it. I can learn to control it and care for myself in healthier ways.

Fast forward to today, our company, HabitAware, has helped hundreds of thousands of people in 80+ countries get better control of their BFRB just like me!

Aneela

For some kids, it might feel like their BFRB is a big part of who they are. But remember, you are so much more than just your BFRB!

Want to know a secret about therapists who help with BFRBs? We're not really focused on whether you pull your hair or pick your skin. What we care about most is helping you make sure your BFRB doesn't stop you from doing what you love and being the person you want to be!

WHAT MATTERS TO ME

Let's explore who you are and what you care about! Take a moment to think about these questions. Some of them might make you think a little deeper.

Who are the people (and pets!) in your life that mean the most to you?

....

....

....

....

....

What is important to you?

....

....

....

....

....

....

What do you like about yourself?

....

....

....

....

....

....

Imagine you hear some kids at school talking about you in a positive way. What would you want them to say about you?

....

....

....

....

....

....

What makes you feel excited?

....

....

....

....

....

....

When you are doing something you love, what do you love about it?

....

....

....

....

....

....

Let's take a closer look at what's important to you. In the illustration in the Creating My Roadmap section below are some examples of *values* that kids might have.

A **value** is something you really care about that helps guide how you want to be. Values aren't goals—goals are things you can check off, like getting an A+ in your math class. Values are more like the things that matter most to you, like being kind or having fun.

For example, you might have a *goal* to learn how to do a back handspring because you *value* being strong, flexible, active, and having fun.

Values are like the direction you're heading on a roadmap, like north on a compass, and goals are the places you want to visit along the way!

Where will *YOUR* roadmap lead?

CREATING MY ROADMAP

Color the values that are important to you and write in other values you have in the blank spaces.

Draw a star ☆ next to the values that are the most important to you.

Draw a check mark ✓ next to the values that you are doing well with now!

Draw two check marks ✓✓ if you are doing very well with this value!

Remember, your values are about what YOU care about, not what your parents or your friends care about!

MY ROADMAP

Being a good sister/brother
Music
Being a good student
Being active or fit
Helping the planet/environment
Being good at sports
Being responsible
Being a good listener
N
Relaxing
Being close with my family
Being knowledgeable
Other value
Other value
FTB ME

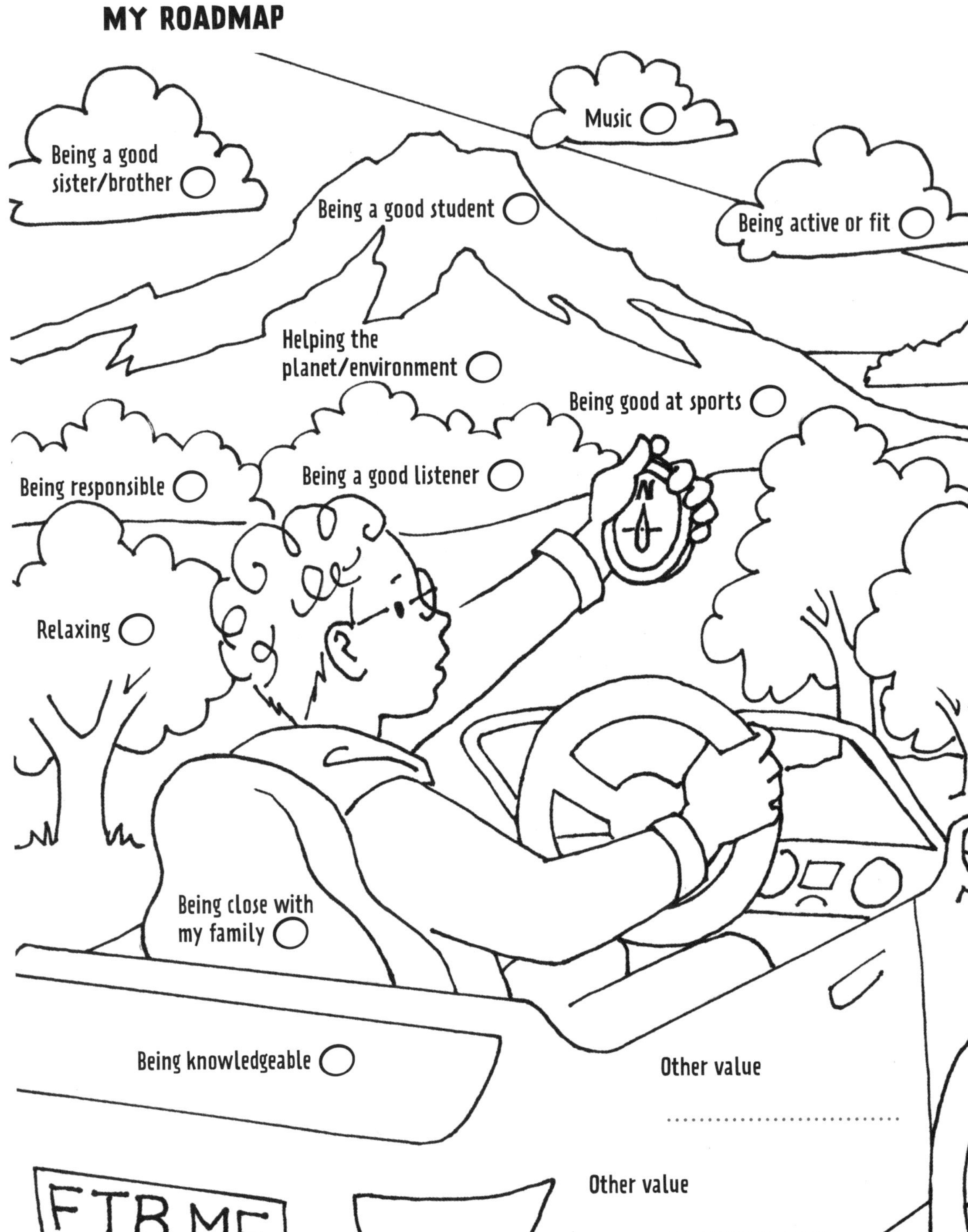

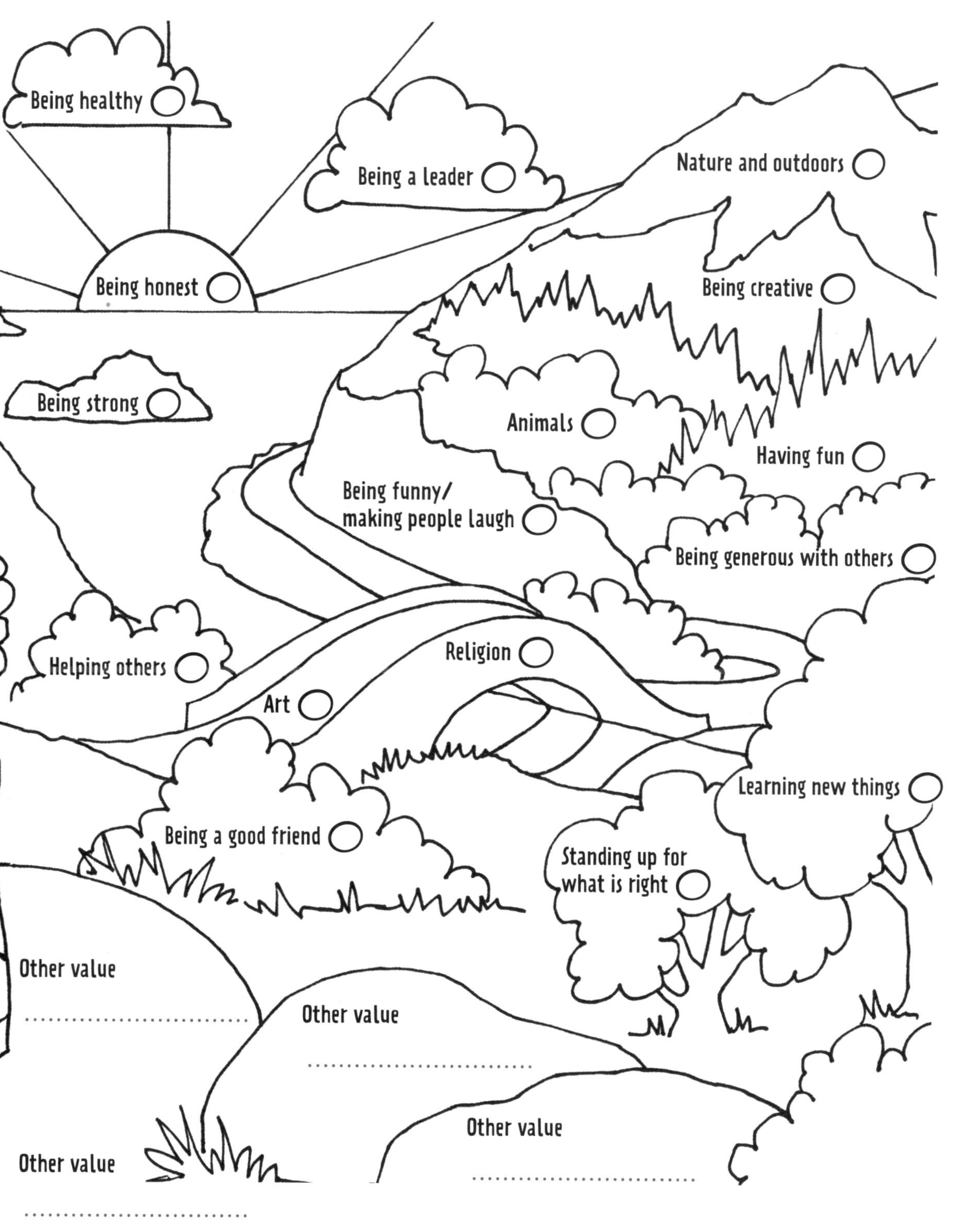
Being healthy
Being a leader
Nature and outdoors
Being honest
Being creative
Being strong
Animals
Having fun
Being funny/
making people laugh
Being generous with others
Religion
Helping others
Art
Learning new things
Being a good friend
Standing up for
what is right
Other value
Other value
Other value
Other value

Great! Now you have an idea of what is important to you.

WHAT GETS IN THE WAY OF ME BEING ME

It would be awesome if we could always be doing the things we care about and the things we want to do. But sometimes, we have to do stuff we don't enjoy, like chores or homework. And other times, we might feel things inside our minds or bodies—like **sensations**, **emotions**, or **thoughts**—that keep us from doing what we care about.

Imagine a cat running toward her food bowl in the kitchen. She's heading straight for what she cares about—eating that tasty food. But then she remembers that she would have to get close to the dog who is sleeping near the food dish, and the dog often likes to chase her! So, she turns and runs the other way, away from the sleeping dog. If we saw the cat running, we may not know if she was running toward something or away from something. But the cat sure does!

Now, let's explore how we humans move toward things or away from them.

When we do things we care about and act the way we want, we're moving toward our values. This is called a "toward move," and it feels good! Take a look at your values again. If I were video recording you, what would I see you doing that shows you're moving toward your values? Let's look at some examples:

Meet Maya and Elliot! Maya is an athletic, energetic kid who enjoys school. She cares about being a good student. A *toward move* for her would be studying hard and finishing her homework.

Elliot is a kind, animal-loving kid who cares about being funny. A *toward move* for him might be telling jokes to his friends.

Another thing about them is that Maya pulls her hair and picks her skin, and Elliot bites his fingernails.

Now let's think about you. Ask a parent to help you find a photo of yourself, cut it out, and paste it onto the circle in the "My Direction" picture on page 44. If you can't find a photo, don't worry—you can always draw yourself!

On the "toward" side of your picture, write the values that are most important to you from pages 36–37. Then, under each one, draw or

write what you *do* when you're living out that value. In the example picture on page 43, Maya drew a picture of herself hugging her mom because her family is important to her. She also drew a picture of herself raising her hand at her school desk because school is important to her.

Next, let's think about the things that pop up in our minds and bodies that can stop us from focusing on what matters most to us. Sometimes, these sensations, emotions, and thoughts are helpful—like the cat remembering the dog, which helped her avoid danger. But other times, they aren't helpful and can feel unwanted! For example, Maya worries about doing badly in school, and Elliot feels strong urges to bite his nails.

Maybe *YOU* have sensations in your body, emotions, or thoughts that bother you and make things harder, just like Maya and Elliot.

Have you ever had thoughts about your BFRB you didn't want, like "People might make fun of me because I don't have eyebrows," or remembering a time when someone actually did make fun of you?

Circle Yes or No.

If you circled "Yes," write them here:

....

....

....

....

Have you ever felt emotions you didn't like, like embarrassment, frustration, or shame?

Circle Yes or No.

If you circled "Yes," write them here:

....

....

....

....

You might have thoughts and emotions that aren't about your BFRB but still bother you a lot. They could be worries about something bad happening, feeling anxious, feeling sad, or remembering things that upset you. Can you think of any of these?

Circle Yes or No.

If you circled "Yes," write them here:

....

....

....

....

Have you ever felt sensations in your body, like an urge to pull your hair, pick your skin, or bite your nails or lips, and it felt uncomfortable? Or maybe you've had an itchy or tingling feeling that you just wanted to stop?

Circle Yes or No.

If you circled "Yes," write them here:

....

....

....

....

When these pesky thoughts, emotions, and sensations pop up, we sometimes try to get rid of them or push them away. Or, we might avoid doing things that could bring up those feelings. And that's totally normal—it's natural to want to stay away from things that make us feel bad.

For example, when Elliot feels the urge to bite his nails, he usually bites for a while to try to make the feeling go away, instead of hanging out and joking with his friends. When Maya worries about getting bad grades, she often pulls her hair, picks her skin, or watches videos instead of doing her homework, even though she cares a lot about doing well in school.

What do you do to get rid of your pesky sensations, emotions, and thoughts?

These are your **away moves**!

Now, on the "away" side of page 44, write down the sensations, emotions, and thoughts that bother you the most. Then, under each one, draw or write what you do to try to get rid of them. In the example picture on page 43, Maya drew her away move, a picture of pulling her hair. She also plays on her device when she has thoughts she doesn't like, so she drew a picture of herself using her device.

MAYA'S DIRECTION

MY DIRECTION

AWAY

TOWARDS

Now, look at your completed My Direction picture. Awesome job finishing this!

Think about how it feels when you take the "toward" road and you are doing those "toward" moves. How does that feel?

Now, think about how it feels when you take the "away" road and you are doing those "away" moves.

When we take the "toward" road, we feel happy and good. But sometimes, we have thoughts, emotions, or sensations we don't like, and we might try to get rid of them. We might try really hard to do this, and sometimes it works, but only for a little while before those thoughts, emotions, or sensations come back.

When we focus so much on trying to get rid of things we don't like, we get stuck on the "away" road and miss out on doing the things that matter to us, just like when Elliot bites his nails instead of hanging out with his friends.

Look at yourself at the fork in the road, and remember, you always have the choice to go toward or away!

THE TRUTH ABOUT BFRBS

Want to know the truth about BFRBs?

Like other "away" moves, your BFRB might make you feel better in the moment, but over time, it can actually make you feel worse and keep you stuck in a loop. Pulling, picking, or biting might get rid of the urge, make you feel calmer, or even out your skin for a bit, but then the urge comes back, or the anxiety comes back, or your skin can feel rough again. Think about the sensations, emotions, or thoughts that bother you the most. Have you ever been able to get rid of one from your mind forever? We bet that you couldn't. They always come back.

But in this book, you'll learn ways to move toward your values—even with those uncomfortable sensations, emotions, or thoughts. And as long as you're willing, moving toward them means becoming the you that you want to be!

Chapter 3

Get to Know My BFRB

"Just Like Me"

By Clare Mackay, PhD, Professor of Imaging Neuroscience, University of Oxford

I started to pull out hair from my head and eyelashes when I was about 12 years old. I don't recall the first time, and I never remember wanting to do it, it just sort of happened. Adolescence is a tricky time for lots of people, and it definitely was for me. My parents separated a couple of years earlier, and I fell victim to some bad bullying when I moved up to high school. When I look back, I think going through these difficulties probably contributed to starting to pull my hair, although I didn't think about that at the time.

Like many children, I also bit my nails. I remember there came a time when my younger sister grew out of her nail biting and I was amazed that she'd been able to stop. I never could, and although it didn't bother me as much as my hair pulling, it did get quite bad sometimes, making me want to hide my hands. The thing that made me feel worse was having no eyelashes. Even though I hated how it made me look, and dreaded that people would notice, I just couldn't leave them alone.

Unfortunately, there wasn't a lot of information available about BFRBs back then, so my parents didn't know how to help me. My Dad thought it was best to ignore it and pretend everything was fine, and my Mum got quite anxious and often told me to "stop it." Neither was very helpful, and I felt very alone in dealing with a lot of shame. My Mum did try to get me help, but the psychologist I saw wasn't very knowledgeable. The only advice I remember getting was not to worry so much about what other people think of me. Not easy for a bullied teenager!

I'm glad we know more about BFRBs now. I recognize mine as a way my body tries to soothe itself. Sometimes that might be because of something stressful, but more often I pick, pull, or bite when I'm just a bit tired or bored. I think that when we beat ourselves up for these behaviors (as I did for years!), we create a greater need to self-soothe, so it's much better to be kind to ourselves. I now recognize the urges as being a message from my body that I need something, and I can look for alternative ways to meet that need. I don't always manage to, but often I do, and I mostly now live with "good enough" eyelashes. BFRBs are not our enemy, they are part of being the unique, awesome humans that we all are.

Clare

MEET MY BFRB BEAST!

Sometimes, BFRBs—like hair pulling, skin picking, or nail biting—feel like they have a mind of their own. It's almost like a little beast that tries to trick you into listening to it. But guess what? *You* are the boss, not the beast! In this activity, you'll draw your own BFRB Beast and give it a name. This will help you understand it better and you might even discover he's kind of interesting!

Close your eyes and think about your BFRB Beast. If it had a shape, what would it look like? Is it big or small? Furry or slimy? Does it have big eyes? Tiny claws? Wings? A silly smile? There are no wrong answers!

Now, grab your markers, crayons, or colored pencils. You might even grab some stickers, googly eyes, or anything fun to decorate your beast and start drawing in the frame on the next page! Make your BFRB Beast look however you imagine it. You can use as many colors and details as you like.

Every beast needs a name! What would you call yours? Write its name at the top of your drawing.

This is ....

Answer these questions about your BFRB Beast:

When does it show up the most? (When you're bored, nervous, watching TV, reading, etc.?)

....

....

....

....

What does it say to make you listen to it?

....

....

....

....

What tricks does it use to get you to do your BFRB?

....

....

....

....

What can you say back to stand up to it?

....

....

....

....

Now that you've met your beast, it's time to take charge! Think of one way you can make your beast *less powerful*. Maybe you can keep your hands busy with a fidget toy, take deep breaths, or tell your monster, "Nope, I'm in charge!"

You can even draw a picture of yourself *shrinking* or *taming* your beast! Give it a try!

Great job! You did it! The more you understand your BFRB Beast, the more power you have over it. Keep your drawing as a reminder that *you* are in control—not the beast!

We have so many more ways to tame your BFRB Beast that we're going to share with you. First, let's get to know it even better!

GET TO KNOW MY BFRB

BFRBs can seem really confusing. Sometimes, it's clear what triggered the behavior, like Maya pulling her hair and picking her skin when she worries about getting good grades, or Elliot biting his nails when he feels an uncomfortable urge.

But other times, it's harder to figure out what triggered the BFRB—it might feel like they just happen, even when you're just trying to fall asleep at night. That's why we're here to help you put on your detective hat and figure out what might seem like a mystery!

MASTER MY A, B, C'S

The key to understanding your BFRB is to learn your A, B, C's! No, not the alphabet song; we know you know that. These are different A, B, C's—the A, B, C's of what makes us do what we do.

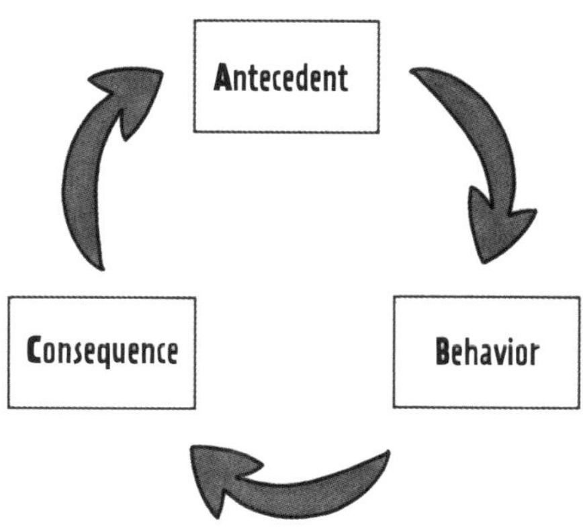

A is for antecedent. Antecedent is a fancy word for trigger. What triggers your BFRB?

B is for behavior. That's an easy one! The behavior is your BFRB.

C is for consequence. That's what happens after you do your BFRB.

Your ABC's work like this: Imagine you notice your stomach grumbling. That doesn't feel good, so you → eat a snack, and after you've eaten, you → feel better—no more grumbling tummy!

In this example,

- your stomach grumbling is the antecedent (the A—the trigger)
- eating a snack is the behavior (the B—the behavior)
- feeling better with no tummy grumbles is the consequence (the C—what happens after the behavior).

And, you're a great learner, so the next time your stomach grumbles, you're probably going to grab that snack to make it feel better. See, these are the A, B, C's of what makes us do what we do. That would look like this:

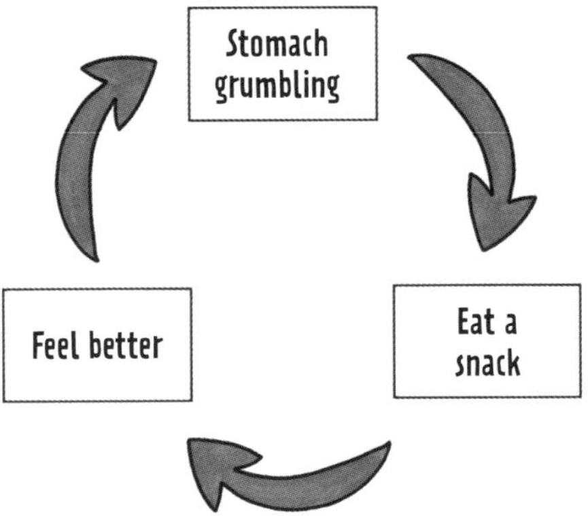

Let's practice! On the next page are some A, B, C's. Draw a check mark "✓" over the A, B, C's you think are correct and draw a cross "X" over the A, B, C's you think are incorrect.

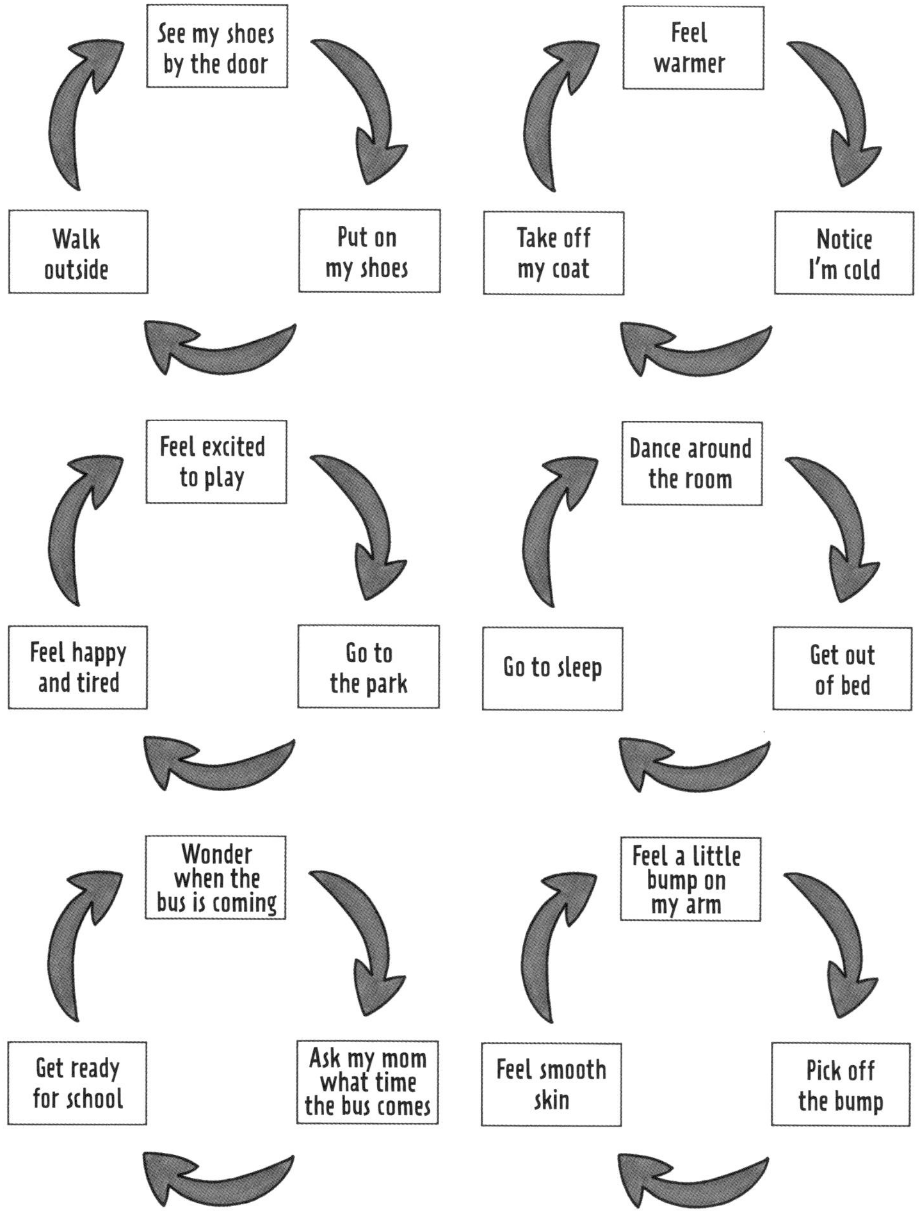

See, this goes for BFRBs too.

When Maya worries (A) → she pulls her hair (B), and → she feels a little bit better to be focusing on her hair instead of her worries (C).

When Elliot feels an urge to bite his nails (A) → he bites his nails (B), and → the urge goes away—he feels better (C).

So, it looks like this:

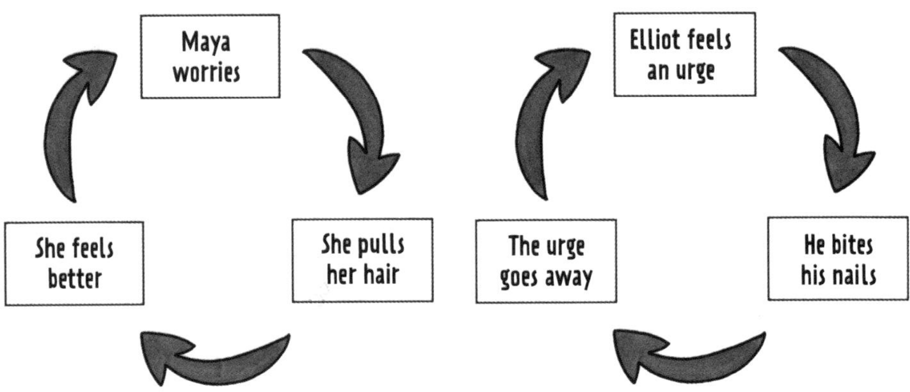

Can you think of the A, B, C's of your BFRB? If you can, write them below:

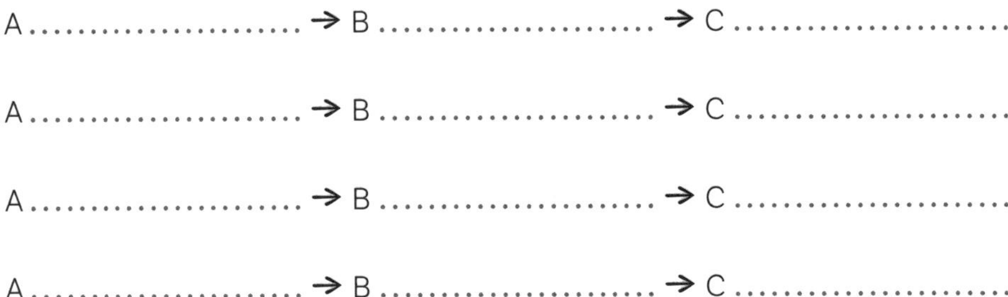

A .... → B .... → C ....

A .... → B .... → C ....

A .... → B .... → C ....

A .... → B .... → C ....

If it's hard to think of your A, B, C's, don't worry! Let's do more detective work to figure them out together.

Analyze My A's

To identify the A's (antecedents), it helps to put on that detective hat, grab that magnifying glass, and look a little bit closer for clues. Here's how we do it:

Discover My 5 W's

Let's look at **the 5 W's—Who, What, When, Where, Why**. You might have heard a teacher say that these are the five things you need to think about if you are planning on writing a story. But THIS story is a story about *YOU*!

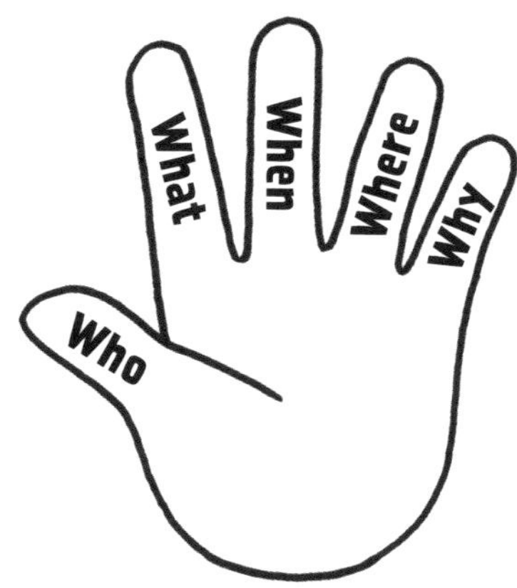

We'll begin with:

Who

The "Who" in your BFRB detective work can be really helpful in solving the mystery of your triggers. Sometimes, kids only do their BFRB when they're alone.

Other times, they might only do it when they're around certain people—sometimes even specific people are around when it happens.

And sometimes, kids do their BFRB whether they're alone or with others.

Think about the questions below and circle the answer or answers that seem right for you:

Are you alone when you do your BFRB?

Yes No Sometimes

Are there other people around you when you do your BFRB?

Yes No Sometimes

If other people are around you, who are the people that are around you when you do your BFRB? Write an "X" next to each one that applies to you.

- ☐ My parent(s)
- ☐ My brother(s) or sister(s)
- ☐ My grandparent(s)
- ☐ My babysitter
- ☐ My teacher
- ☐ My friend(s)

Who are the other people that are around you when you do your BFRB? Draw them or write their names below:

What?

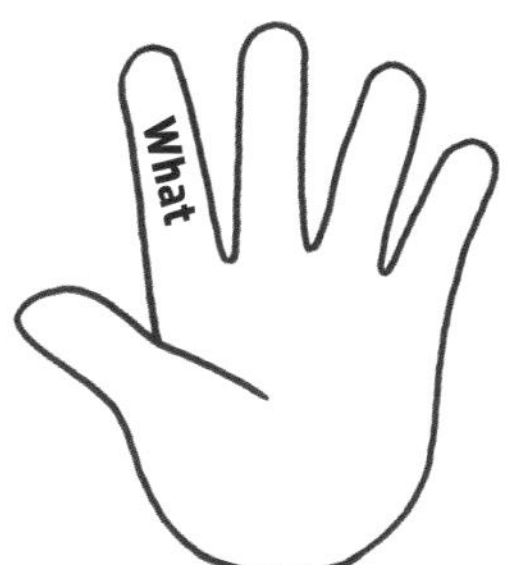

The "What" in your BFRB detective work is also important for solving the mystery of your triggers! Sometimes, kids do their BFRB more often when certain things are around them or when they're doing certain activities.

For example, some kids might do their BFRB more when they look in a mirror while brushing their hair or when they are cutting their nails. Other kids might do it when they're doing homework, watching TV, or using their iPad.

Think about these questions and draw or write the answers that feel right for you: What's around you when you do your BFRB? What are you doing at the time? Picture where you are when it happens and think about what you're doing and what you see around you.

For example, if you're in your bedroom, maybe you're doing your homework with your bed and desk nearby. If you're in the bathroom, maybe you're brushing your hair with a bathroom mirror in front of you. Or, if you're in your classroom, maybe you're doing classwork with your desk, the whiteboard, and your pencil box around you.

So, using your imagination, what's around you when you do your BFRB?

When?

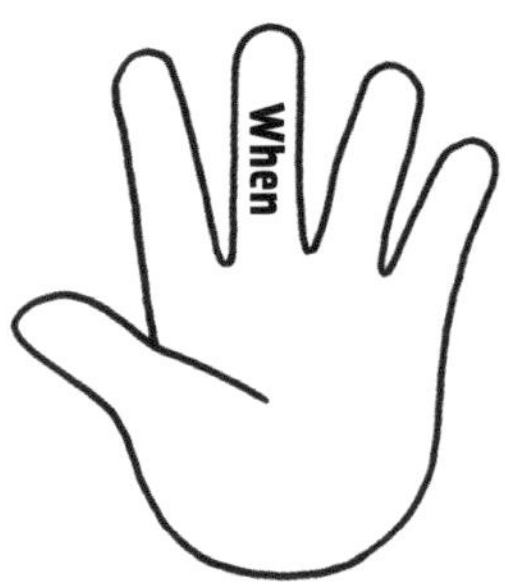

Don't forget about the "When" in your BFRB detective work—that's another clue! Sometimes, kids do their BFRB more often at certain times of the day, like at night after a long day or in the morning when they're rushing to get ready for school. If you do your BFRB at more than one time during the day, that's helpful information too!

Think about this question and draw or write the answers that seem right for you:

Is there a particular time of day when you do your BFRB? Show us in a drawing.

Where?

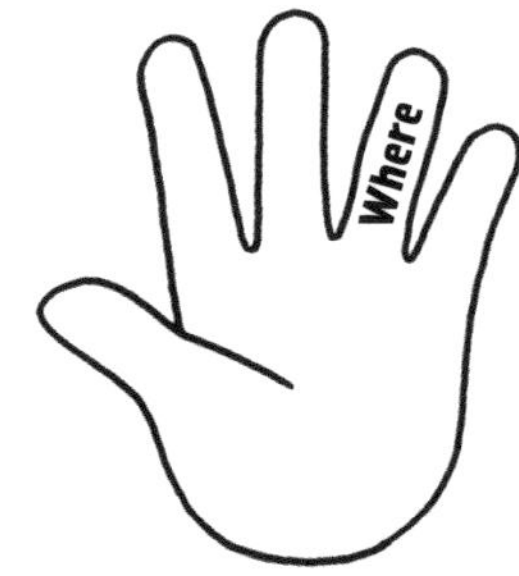

The fourth "W" is "Where." Sometimes, kids do their BFRB more often in a specific place, like riding in the car, laying in their bed at night, or standing on the sidelines of the soccer field getting ready to play the game with their team.

Where you are can be very important.

For example, Maya pulls her hair when she's lying in her bed. Elliot bites his nails when he's sitting at his desk.

The "Where" is like the board in a board game—you can't play some games very easily without the board!

Think about where you are when you do your BFRB.

Think about this question and draw or write the answers that seem right for you:

Why?

The "Why" in your BFRB detective work can be a little tricky. But hang in there—these are your last clues to the mystery!

Think about your favorite board game, like Monopoly, Checkers, Guess Who?, or another game you like to play. To play the game, you need to set up the board and set out the pieces on the board, right? It's hard to play a game without setting it up first.

It makes it much easier, and it might even make us want to play the game to see it set up for us!

Explore My SET Up

Now, let's think about your BFRB. "Why" is your BFRB being SET up? Hmmmmm... Why? Let's look at the **SET** up:

ensations

motions

houghts

The "S" is for **Sensations**.

Sensations are the feelings in your body, like a tickle, an itch, or an urge. For example, Maya picks her skin when she feels the sensation of a raised bump on her skin. That's one of her Why's.

Think about this question and draw or write the answers that feel right for you: Do you notice any sensations right before you do your BFRB? How does your body feel? Write or draw your answers below:

The "E" stands for **Emotions**.

Emotions are the feelings we have, and there are so many different ones! You can feel a lot of different emotions before doing your BFRB, and that can be a little confusing. That's why we need to do some detective work!

For example, Elliot bites his fingernails when he feels bored.

Look at the faces below and color in the faces that are feeling the emotions that you sometimes feel before you do your BFRB.

Great job!

Are there other emotions that you sometimes feel before your BFRB that aren't shown above? Draw your own faces showing those emotions below.

The "T" is for **THOUGHTS**.

Thoughts are the words we're thinking in our minds. If you're like us, you probably have thoughts running through your head all the time—thoughts about what you're feeling, what you're doing, and what you'll be doing later. So many thoughts!

Here's a fun fact: Did you know people have thousands of thoughts every day? Yep, they do—and you do, too!

Thoughts can be really important when it comes to BFRBs because they can set them up and make them more likely to happen.

For example, Maya pulls her hair or picks her skin when she's thinking about school and worrying about her grades. It's something she does when she feels worried. Hmmmm... time to get your detective gear on and check out your thoughts!

What kind of thoughts do you have before your BFRB? Color in the thought bubbles of the kids who are having thoughts just like yours.

"This scab needs to go."

"I can't stop doing my BFRB."

"They won't want to be my friend if they know I have a BFRB."

"I'm going to stop this BFRB right now from now on."

"What if I can't stop my BFRB?"

"My hair will never grow back if I keep doing this."

"Will anyone notice this bald spot?"

"I'm going to stop doing my BFRB after I just do it for a few minutes."

"I need to get this hair!"

"My parents would be upset with me if they knew I just picked my skin."

"I bit off one nail, I might as well bite the rest of them."

"I can't stand this rough skin on the bottom of my feet."

"I wonder if I can get one of those chunky hair roots again if I pull this hair."

"I wonder if I am the only one who eats my scabs."

"I wish I could keep doing this and my hair would instantly grow back."

"I can't stand it when my eyebrows look bushy."

"If I pick that, it will heal faster."

Are there other thoughts before you do your BFRB? Write those thoughts in the bubbles below:

Awesome job! You've gathered a lot of clues! Add the clues you've found to the chart below. Try to notice your BFRB this week and add any new clues you discover. Write your name at the top and keep track of what you notice. You can even ask a parent to help you collect the clues!

5 W's Chart

Understanding My BFRB

Who is around me?	**What** am I doing and what is around me?	**When** is this happening?	**Where** am I?	**Why** is my BFRB being **SET** up?
My mom	*Watching TV, sitting on the sofa*	*In the evening, after dinner*	*In the family room*	**S**(ensations): Itchy sensation on the head **E**(motions): Tired **T**(houghts): "I need to get rid of this itch." "This feels good."
				S(ensations): .... **E**(motions): .... **T**(houghts): ....
				S(ensations): .... **E**(motions): .... **T**(houghts): ....
				S(ensations): .... **E**(motions): .... **T**(houghts): ....
				S(ensations): .... **E**(motions): .... **T**(houghts): ....

You're on your way to solving the mystery!!

Bring Attention to My B's

Now that you are more aware of your A's—your antecedents, or triggers—let's look at the **Behavior** part of your BFRB to see what else you can learn. There may be times you will be super aware of your BFRB and there may be times that it feels like it occurs when you are zoned out.

You may notice certain **S**ensations, **E**motions, or **T**houghts that occur *during* your BFRB as well as before it. There are three main parts to a BFRB behavior:

Search → Action → Disposal

The Search—looking for the exact spot or special thing about your hair, skin, or nails

The Action—how you do your BFRB

The Disposal—what you do with the hair, skin, or nails after

The Search—A BFRB often begins with searching for a spot to pick, pull, or bite.

For Maya, it starts with her hands gently stroking her hair and, before long, she finds herself searching for rough hairs or split ends. When her fingers brush against a bumpy, rough hair at the top of her head, she instinctively thinks, "This one's different, it has to go."

Elliot notices that he tends to pinch his fingers together and rub his nails on his thumb, looking for any rough or jagged edges. When he feels a particularly uneven nail, a wave of discomfort rises up his spine.

Do you have a specific area of your body where your BFRB is most active?

Is there something about your hair, skin, or nails that draws your attention?

How do you catch yourself looking for that hair, skin, or nail spot to pull, pick, or bite?

What do you think you're searching for at that moment?

The Action—Once your brain and hands find what they're looking for, what comes next? This is the *Action* phase of your BFRB.

Pay close attention to the specific steps you take—how do you remove the hair, skin, or nails?

Take note of:

- which hand you use
- whether you rely on a mirror or tools
- if you focus on one area or move between multiple spots
- how long the behavior lasts
- how absorbed you are in the action
- what finally brings the episode to an end.

....

....

....

....

For example, Elliot notices a rough nail and instinctively feels it with his tongue. He then uses his front teeth to bite off the rough edge. Next, he picks up his pen, pressing it against his cuticles and nails to lift any loose skin or jagged edges. Fascinated by the behavior, he pays little attention to his surroundings. He continues examining each fingernail, one by one, stopping only when he has smoothed out all the rough spots and suddenly becomes more aware of the show he's watching.

Now, put on your detective hat and carefully map out what you do during your BFRB action. Write down every step involved in your BFRB—each movement, tool, and trigger that contributes. The more specific and detailed, the better!

....

....

....

....

The Disposal—Finally, let's think about what happens after you do your BFRB—what do you do with the hair, skin, or nails once they've been removed? Everyone has different ways of handling it. Some people might pull and toss, or pick and flick, while others do something special with the hair, skin, or nails once they've removed them. This part of the BFRB can feel like you're doing something unique, but actually, lots of people around the world do similar things. For example, Maya gets excited when she pulls a hair and finds a little bulb at the end. She likes to stick it to the back of her hand, rub it on her lips, then bite it off and swallow it. After that, she plays with the hair for a bit and then drops it on the floor. Sometimes, when she pulls a lot of hairs, she hides them in her trash can.

What do you do with your hair, skin, or nails after your BFRB happens? Do you have a special way of handling them?

....

....

....

....

It is not unusual to chew, eat, or swallow hair, but if your hair is long, in very rare cases, it could cause a tummy problem that needs to be checked by a medical doctor. This is called a trichobezoar, and it can make a hairball form in your stomach, which could block your digestion. The good news is, it can be treated and removed! So, if you've swallowed some long hair and you feel any tummy pain or have trouble going to the bathroom, it's really important to tell an adult or doctor.

The more you understand about your BFRB, the more you'll know which skills you can practice helping your body and curious mind find other ways to feel better. Did you notice any changes in how you felt, what you thought, or how your body reacted when your BFRB went through the search, the action, and the disposal? What else did you learn about your BFRB?

....

....

....

....

Search → Action → Disposal		
Search	**Action**	**Disposal**
Reading at night and fingers wander to explore and rub eyebrows. **S**(ensations): Touching pokey hairs **E**(motions): Annoyed **T**(houghts): "I need to get rid of this one, it feels different"	Pinch my pointer finger and thumb on my right hand to pull out a pokey eyebrow. Go into the bathroom and get tweezers to get the short stubby hairs. **S**(ensations): It feels good to pull out the brow hair, especially the thick ones. **E**(motions): Satisfied **T**(houghts): "This feels good, and I don't want to stop"	Once the hair is pulled, I like to look closely at the hair and stick it to my book or the back of my hand. **S**(ensations): I like the sticky feeling at the end of the eyebrow hair **E**(motions): Interested **T**(houghts): "I like the feeling of these hairs on my hand, and they look interesting on the white paper"

Now, you try it.

Search → Action → Disposal		
Search	**Action**	**Disposal**

Catch My C's

Finally, let's take a closer look at the C's—the **Consequences** of doing your BFRB. We'll talk about what happens right after you do your BFRB and what can happen later.

First, let's focus on the Sensations, Emotions, and Thoughts (SET) that happen after you do your BFRB.

After doing a BFRB, people often feel different **Sensations** in their body, and sometimes these feelings can be nice, which makes them want to do it again.

For example, when Maya picks her skin, it feels smooth, which gives her some relief. But after a while, she starts to feel her skin getting rough again.

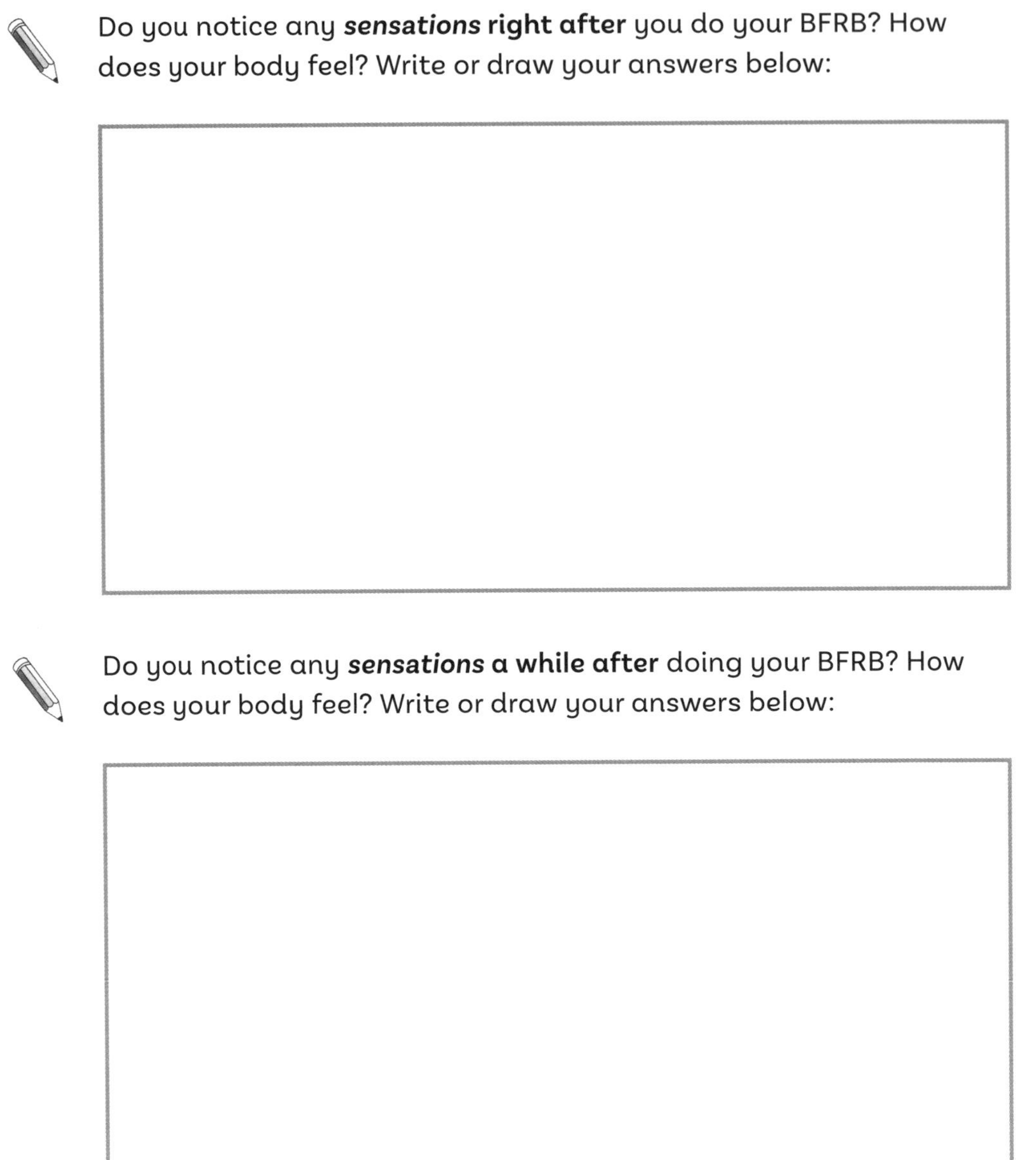

Do you notice any ***sensations* right after** you do your BFRB? How does your body feel? Write or draw your answers below:

Do you notice any ***sensations* a while after** doing your BFRB? How does your body feel? Write or draw your answers below:

Many different **Emotions** can come up after you do your BFRB too!

After Elliot bites his nails, he feels energized and satisfied. People can feel all sorts of emotions after doing their BFRB, like happy, calm, relieved, or even angry or frustrated.

Which ***emotions*** do you feel **right after** you do your BFRB? Write or draw your answers below:

Which ***emotions*** do you feel **a while after** doing your BFRB? Write or draw your answers below:

You can also have lots of different **Thoughts** after doing your BFRB.

For example, Maya often thinks "This feels so good" as soon as she pulls her hair, but then after a while she has thoughts like "My hair will never grow back if I keep pulling it" or "Will anyone notice this bald spot?"

What are some thoughts you have immediately after you do your BFRB? Write those thoughts in the bubbles below:

What are some thoughts you have a few minutes, a few hours, or a few days later because you did your BFRB? Write those thoughts in the bubbles below:

The sensations, emotions, and thoughts are what happen **inside** your mind and body after you do your BFRB. But what happens on the **outside**? What happens to your behavior or the way other people behave?

For example, Elliot tries to hide his nails after he bites them. Some kids might cover up bald spots in their hair by wearing different hairstyles or a hat. Others might avoid swimming because they don't want people to see scabs or scars from picking. Some kids might even find that after doing their BFRB, they end up arguing with their parents or caregivers.

Are there things that you do, or other people do, after you do your BFRB? Write or draw your answers below:

Great work. Now you know your C's!

Think about everything you've learned that happens after you do your BFRB. A lot of people feel good right after they pick or pull! It can feel nice to get rid of rough skin or pull out a thick hair.

But then, they might start feeling bad or have thoughts they don't like, and it might even stop them from doing things they enjoy. It's really important to notice these **Consequences** because sometimes these uncomfortable feelings or thoughts can make them want to do the BFRB again. For example, if they feel guilty about having made a bald spot by pulling hair from a specific spot, that guilt can feel pretty bad. And sometimes that bad feeling might make kids want to do their BFRB to make them feel better.

And then, they get stuck in the ABC loop, going round and round! Do you notice this pattern?

Now, you have more clues to understand your A, B, C's!! Let's write out *your* A, B, C's of your BFRB now. Write your name on the chart and fill in the A, B, C's in the boxes on the A, B, C's chart on the following page.

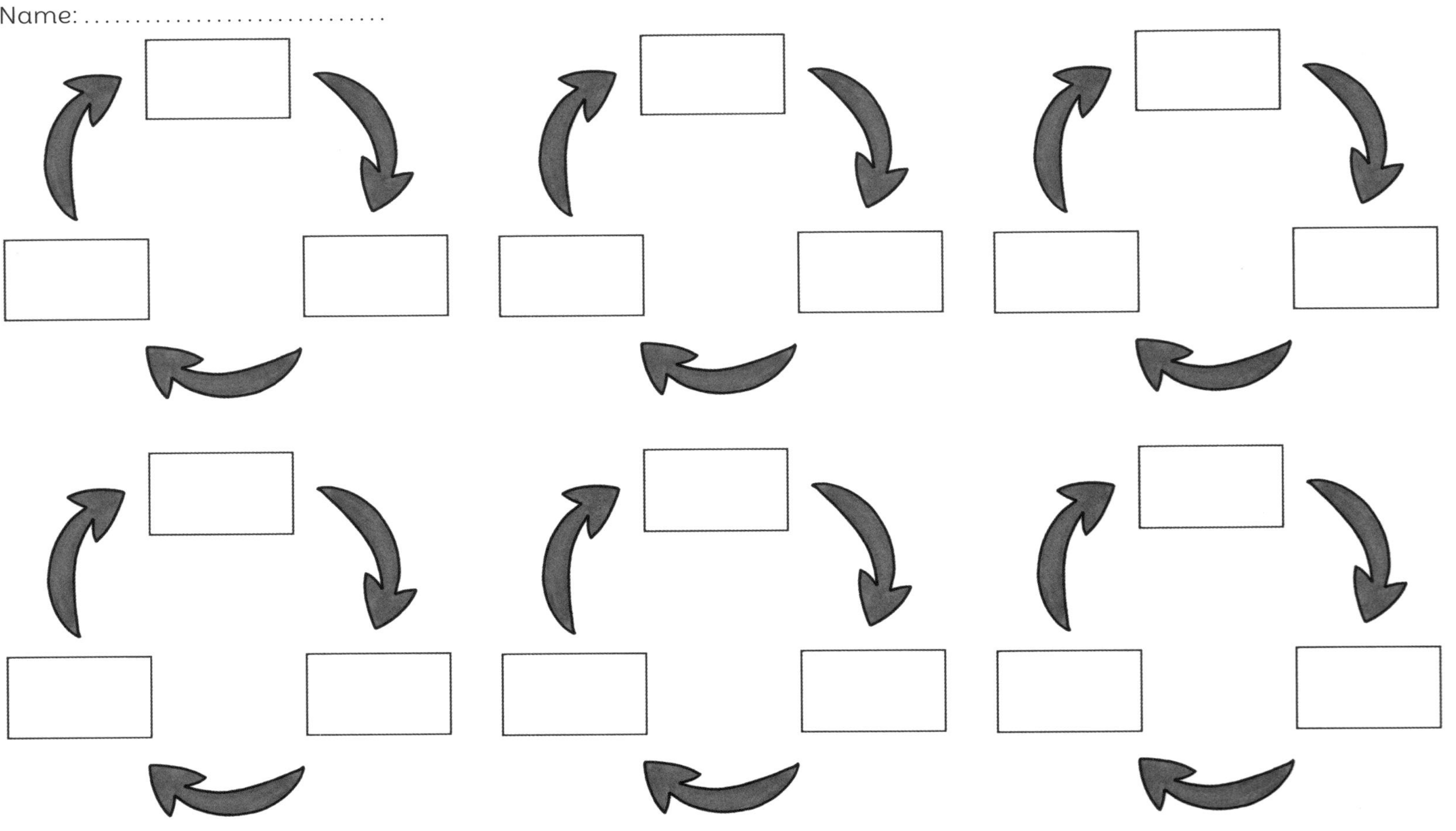
Name: ....

Part II

GET SET

Chapter 4

Healthy Bodies, Healthy Minds

"Just Like Me"

By Gessie Perez, Author and BFRB Advocate

When I was 11 years old, I started pulling the hair on my head. I didn't know why I did it, only that it felt good. A few years later, I also started plucking my eyebrows. By the time I was in high school, I developed large bald spots on my head and was missing most of my eyebrows. I tried to hide my hair loss with ponytails, big headbands, and makeup. At one point, I even shaved my head and started wearing a wig.

I eventually found out there was a name for my hair pulling: trichotillomania. But I was still so embarrassed and ashamed about it. It felt like nobody understood what I was going through.

Then at the age of 16, my mom took me to a conference for people with body-focused repetitive behaviors (BFRBs), like hair pulling and skin picking. It was life changing. I learned different coping strategies, and my mom learned how to support me better. Best of all, I got to meet other kids who understood me, and for the first time ever, I didn't feel alone.

Knowing that I wasn't alone gave me the courage and freedom to be myself. I stopped hiding my hair loss, and told all my friends and extended family about my trichotillomania. I wanted to raise my voice so that other people wouldn't feel alone. I started sharing my story anywhere I could and raising awareness for BFRBs.

Now, as a grown-up, I still pull my hair, but it doesn't make me sad like it once used to. I don't let trichotillomania stop me from doing anything I set my mind to! I have written two books about my life with trichotillomania. I started my own mentorship program for young girls, called Trichster Sisters. I also lead support groups for kids with BFRBs. I am dedicated to giving back to the BFRB community, because I don't want other kids to grow up feeling ashamed and alone like I did. Growing up with BFRBs can be hard, but I truly believe we are more special and strong because of it.

Gessie

Now that you have become a great detective and learned all about your BFRB, let's learn about how to manage it so it doesn't steer you away from the life you want to live and the person you want to be!

Think of yourself as an awesome race car. Many kids with BFRBs are built like a high-performance race car, and you may need to take extra good care of yourself to run at your best! Like a powerful race car, you might need to learn a few things to best drive yourself through life. Here, you will learn to take care of your body and mind through proper sleep, nutrition, positive relationships, and other cool self-care tips!

Before we start our driving lessons, take a minute and draw yourself as a fancy race car. You got some power under that hood!

A race car doesn't run smoothly if it doesn't have good fuel, has a flat tire, or is overheated! It's out of balance and needs certain stuff to run well. BFRBs can happen when people are out of balance too. By taking care of your mind and body in healthy ways, you can help your BFRB show up less often and make the urge to do it weaker.

SLEEP

Even the fastest race cars need to take a break and cool down. For people, this is where sleep comes in! Our bodies do amazing things while we sleep to help us recharge and get ready to be our best. When we don't get enough sleep, our bodies can't do this important work, and we might start feeling tired and low on energy. Many kids do their BFRBs right before bed because they're trying to relax, feel exhausted, or have trouble falling asleep.

Let's explore your sleep habits.

What time do you go to bed at night? What time do you wake up in the morning? Math alert... how many total hours of sleep are you getting?

....

....

....

....

Do you usually keep the same bedtime and wake up time or does it bounce around?

....

....

....

....

Do you have a hard time falling asleep? How long does it take?

....

....

....

....

Do you sleepwalk, have to use the bathroom at night, or have wild or scary dreams?

....

....

....

....

Is there anything about your room that makes it hard to sleep at night? Do you share a room with a snoring sibling? Have fears about the dark? Have noises that keep you awake?

....

....

....

....

How tired do you feel in the morning? Do you nap during the day? Do you fall asleep at school or during other activities?

....

....

....

....

When you do not get enough sleep, what do you notice about your feelings and behaviors?

....

....

....

....

Do you think too little or too much sleep has an impact on your BFRB?

....

....

....

....

If you're like almost all other humans, you will notice that how much you sleep and how well you sleep will influence your mind and body.

Fun fact: Kids need about ten hours of sleep per night to allow their bodies to do the important work of brain and body development!

Sleep ideas: If sleep is a problem for you, here are some great ideas to get your engine running better:

- ✓ Create a bedtime routine. Each night, try to put on your pajamas, brush your teeth, and go to bed around the same time. It is also good to try to wake up around the same time—even on the weekends.
- ✓ Try to resist eating a big meal right before bed. Digestion takes a lot of work, and it can cause you to not sleep as well.
- ✓ Try to exercise earlier in the afternoon so your body isn't too hyped up right before bed. Bedtime is a great time to relax and calm your body down.
- ✓ Try to sleep in your room rather than on a sofa or in a place where there is bright light, other people running around, or a lot of noise.

- ✓ Turn off your video games, computer, phone, and TV at least one hour before bed. The light from these screens tends to trick our brains into thinking it is daytime and can keep us awake.

- ✓ Make your sleep space relaxing and comfortable. If there is something about your sleep space that makes you feel scared or unsafe, talk to an adult that you trust to help you.

Think about the sleep tips above. Are there any other ways that you can improve your sleep? What is one small step you can try to do this week?

....

....

....

....

....

....

....

....

NUTRITION: FOOD AS FUEL

Next time you're at a gas station, look at the gas pump. You'll see that there are different types of gasoline. Fancy cars need the best fuel to run well, and they don't do so great on the cheap stuff. The same goes for your body! If you're eating a lot of fast food or sugary snacks (like candy), you might start to feel yucky if you eat too much. Some people find that their BFRB can show up when they've eaten too much of the "cheap stuff" and can make them feel tired, unfocused, or even have a stomachache.

It's a good idea to try eating foods from all the food groups and try new things that help your body and mind grow healthy and strong. If you're not sure what's healthy or not, ask your parents, health teacher, doctor, or a dietitian. They'll help you figure it out, and you'll be glad you asked!

This is an example of what our food choices and amounts of food should look like:

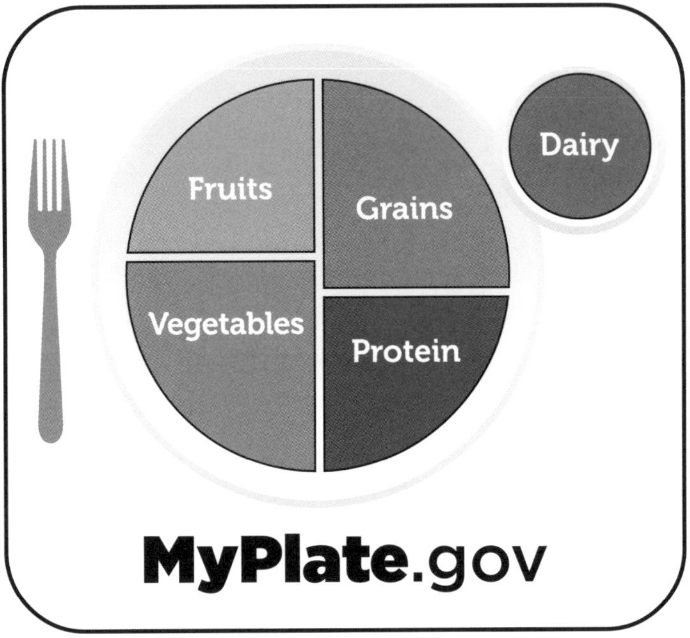

Draw a picture of a meal that you have often and enjoy.

What are some of your favorite healthy foods? How often do you eat them?

....

....

....

....

What are some of your favorite unhealthy foods? How often do you eat them?

....

....

....

....

How many meals do you eat each day? How many snacks?

....

....

....

....

Do you think you are not eating enough, eating too much, or taking in certain types of foods in unhealthy amounts?

....

....

....

....

....

Nutrition ideas:

- ✓ Every day, try to eat breakfast, lunch, and dinner around the same time. Having some small snacks in between can also be good for a growing body.
- ✓ Eat a variety of healthy, brightly colored foods. Brightly colored fruits and vegetables tend to have the best food fuel. Eat the rainbow!
- ✓ Remember to drink water and limit drinks with a lot of sugar or caffeine, like soda.
- ✓ Be adventurous and try new foods! If your taste buds aren't used to eating the healthy stuff, try to add seasoning, cheese, dips, or dressings that you like. With practice, your body will crave veggies and fruits.
- ✓ If you are not sure about what you eat, you can keep a food diary to monitor your eating habits.
- ✓ Know that it is okay to have some junk food, or cheap fuel. They are "sometimes foods" as treats. Just don't fill your whole tank on it every day!

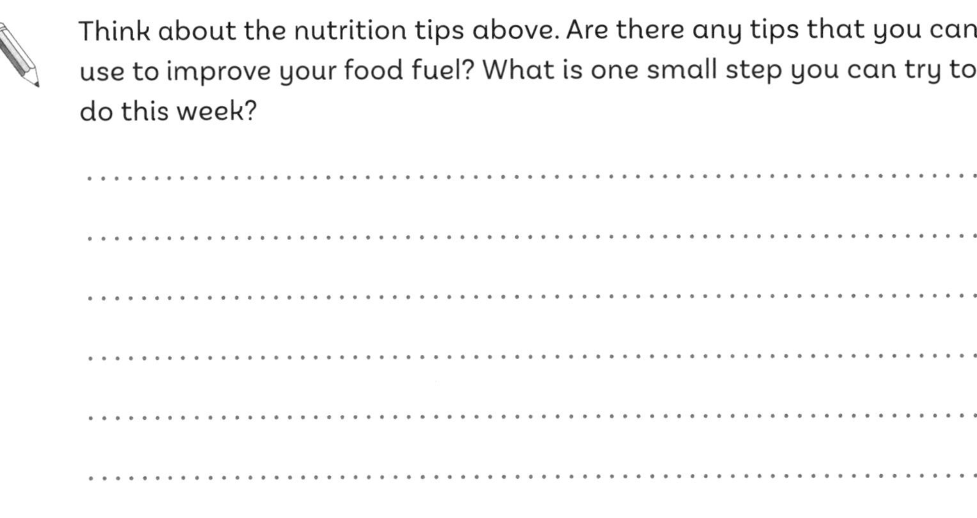

Think about the nutrition tips above. Are there any tips that you can use to improve your food fuel? What is one small step you can try to do this week?

EXERCISE: START YOUR ENGINES!

Exercise is a super way to help your body feel more balanced! Lots of people say that moving their body helps decrease the urge to do their BFRB. There are many reasons for this, like how exercise can improve your mood, give you more oxygen, boost your blood flow, and even help get rid of toxins from your body through breathing, sweating, and better digestion. All of this helps refresh your body, giving you more energy and making you feel happier! How cool is that?

There are so many fun ways to get your body moving and grooving!

See how many words describing exercise or physical activities you can find in this word search!

C	X	S	U	U	S	T	R	E	T	C	H	P	N	U
H	Y	K	G	S	K	C	T	T	S	K	I	I	N	G
E	G	A	P	W	B	F	O	O	T	B	A	L	L	A
E	Y	T	H	I	U	A	L	O	H	O	C	K	E	Y
R	M	E	J	M	N	N	D	A	T	Q	Q	R	W	R
L	N	B	W	S	D	G	S	M	C	E	W	U	A	O
E	A	O	R	R	K	A	P	O	I	R	R	N	L	W
A	S	A	E	K	T	I	N	O	F	N	O	I	K	I
D	T	R	S	O	A	E	P	C	N	T	T	S	N	N
I	I	D	T	S	S	R	N	P	E	G	B	O	S	G
N	C	I	L	O	Q	N	A	N	I	Q	B	A	N	E
G	S	N	I	C	S	K	A	T	I	N	G	P	L	L
Q	Y	G	N	C	Y	O	G	A	E	S	G	D	A	L
U	P	S	G	E	G	O	L	F	F	H	I	K	E	T
B	I	K	E	R	E	B	A	S	E	B	A	L	L	O

Badminton	Dance	Hike	Ping pong	Skateboarding	Soccer	Tennis
Baseball	Football	Hockey	Rowing	Skating	Softball	Walk
Bike	Golf	Karate	Run	Skiing	Stretch	Wrestling
Cheerleading	Gymnastics	Lacrosse	Scootering	Skipping	Swim	Yoga

What other activity words would you add to this list?

....

....

....

....

....

What are some of your favorite physical activities?

....

....

....

....

....

How often do you get your body moving during the week?

....

....

....

....

....

Do you notice that moving too little or too much tends to increase your BFRB?

....

....

....

....

....

Exercise ideas:

- ✓ If you're not used to exercising, start small and set goals that feel doable. Don't try to run a marathon in your first week! Instead, try dancing to your favorite music or taking your dog for a walk around the block.
- ✓ Keep track of how much you're moving and how it makes you feel!
- ✓ Make a plan! If you already play a sport, you might have regular exercise built into your routine. If not, try making your own workout schedule. You can be flexible and get creative with it!
- ✓ Find activities that you enjoy. Exercise should not be a punishment; have some fun!
- ✓ Talk to your parents or doctor if you have any injuries or physical conditions that make it difficult or unsafe for you to exercise.

Think about all of the ways to exercise and move your body. What are some ways you like to exercise and move your body? What is one small step you can try to do this week?

....

....

....

....

....

....

....

....

....

PHYSICAL AND EMOTIONAL CARE: READ YOUR OWNER'S MANUAL

If you have any physical conditions that make you more tired, cause skin problems, or if you find that you're sensitive to certain foods, you might notice that your BFRB happens more when you're not feeling your best. Sometimes, kids with BFRBs experience hair loss or damage to their nails, lips, cheeks, or skin. This can make them feel uncomfortable, itchy, or even hurt. And sometimes, these physical sensations can make you want to pick, pull, or bite more. A lot of kids get frustrated with this loop. Have you noticed this happening to you?

Some people might have stronger feelings from the start, or big life events might have shaped how they react to certain situations. You might not have learned the best ways to take care of your emotions right away, and sometimes, those feelings can build up over time. Did you know that about half of mental health conditions like anxiety, ADHD, Tourette syndrome, OCD, and depression start when people are kids? So, if you have one or more of these, you're not alone—lots of kids feel the same way!

Just like how your BFRB can affect your body, it can also bring up different emotions. Some feelings might be good at first, like feeling proud of pulling the perfect hair ("Yeah, I pulled the perfect hair!"), but later you might feel upset, guilty, or frustrated with yourself ("Oh man, I can't believe I did that"). These feelings can make your BFRB happen more, and it can feel like you're stuck in a loop. But the cool part is, if you can notice these feelings, there are lots of helpful skills to break the loop and feel better!

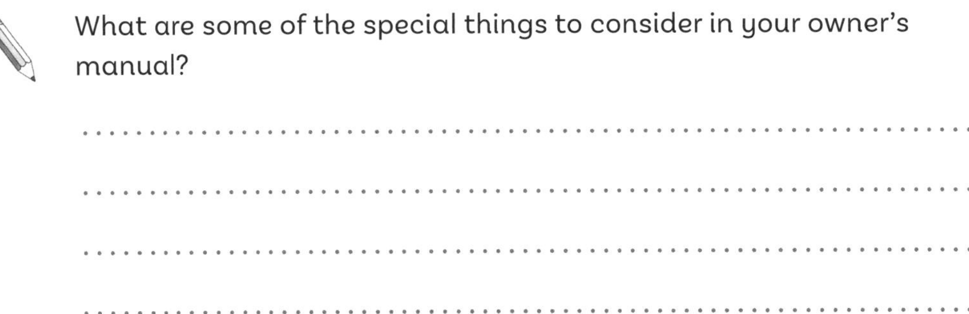

Do you have any physical/medical conditions? If so, how would you describe them?

....

....

....

....

How do you care for yourself if you have any physical/medical conditions?

....

....

....

....

How big do your emotions feel? Do you find it hard to feel them, do they feel like they're in the middle, or do they come on super strong?

....

....

....

....

Have you had any big life experiences that changed your physical or emotional health? If so, did those experiences change how you react in certain situations?

....

....

....

....

Do you currently have any situations that are stressing you out?

How do you take care of your feelings? What are some ways that help you feel better when you're upset? Are there any ways you deal with your emotions that don't work so well?

If you have a physical or mental health condition, how do you think this impacts your BFRB? Does this physical or emotional condition get worse after you do your BFRB behavior?

Physical and emotional care ideas:

- ✓ Listen to your body. If you notice you get sick after eating certain foods or feel tired all the time even when you get enough sleep, then it might be good to have a chat with your parent(s) or doctor.
- ✓ Listen to your emotional health needs. If you notice that you cannot shake feelings of sadness, anxiety, or are having a

really hard time learning or focusing, then it would be good to talk to a parent or a professional who can help.

- ✓ Understand that with a fancy body and mind, you'll sometimes need a team of professionals to help you learn how to best care for yourself. That may include your pediatrician, medication provider, dermatologist, allergist, psychologist, and any other professionals you may need. Think of these people as your pit stop crew on the racetrack!

- ✓ Remember to practice self-love and good self-care as you learn more about your body and mind.

- ✓ Follow the recommendations and treatments that your doctors recommend. It takes work to learn how to best drive your body and mind, and you are worth it!

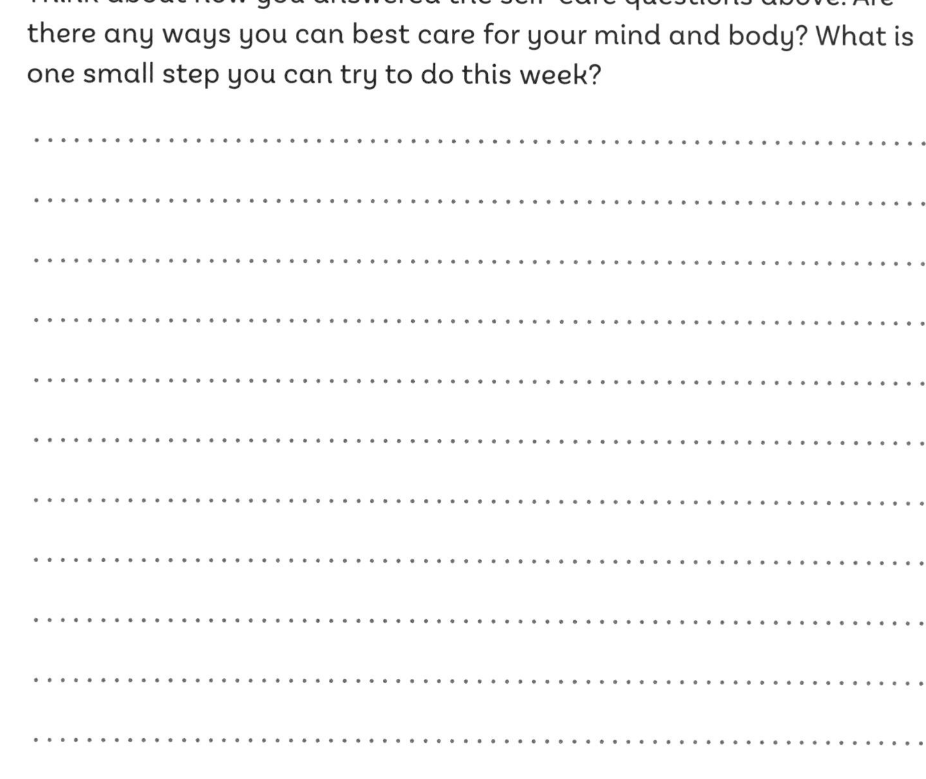

Think about how you answered the self-care questions above. Are there any ways you can best care for your mind and body? What is one small step you can try to do this week?

Chapter 5

Create My BFRB Toolbox

"Just Like Me"

By Michael Herold, former Cartoon Animator, now Confidence Coach, Co-Host of Psychologists Off the Clock podcast

I remember sitting in the backseat of my Dad's car when I was six years old. My Dad was the coolest person I knew—he was funny, strong, and a good friend (he still is).

But in the car, I watched him do something that no one else was doing: he would bite on a fingernail for a while and then spit it out of the window! And because my Dad was so cool, I started doing it too.

In the beginning, it felt a bit strange to me. I only did it when I had a fingernail that was too long. I knew the proper way to do it was to use a nail clipper. But to be like my Dad, I had to bite the long nail off! It was a bit awkward at first because I didn't know how to do it. But over time, I learned to look for small cracks and notches in my fingernails. These made it easy to take a piece of my nail off.

Then something else happened: I started to enjoy it when I was picking my nails. It wasn't important if they were long or short. It was important that they were straight and without any cracks, so I was always checking that all my nails were smooth. I noticed that this was very relaxing and that it could distract me when I was nervous. So, from then on, whenever I was nervous or stressed, for example in a class I didn't like, I would go and pick my nails. It would make me feel a little better for a short time.

Now that I am grown up, I still find myself biting my nails and picking them too. When I am not using my hands for something, like writing, eating, or playing a video game, then my fingers are probably picking at each other. But it has become much easier to handle. I have learned that if I take care of my nails, then there is not so much reason to pick them.

I have also learned that when I am nervous or stressed, there are much better things to do than picking my nails because that never makes it any better.

Michael

MY BFRB TOOLBOX

Now that you have learned how to take care of your body and mind like a fancy race car, let's fill up your BFRB Toolbox with all the tools you'll need to run smoothly!

Have you ever built or fixed something before? You usually need lots of different tools! Sometimes you need a hammer, sometimes a screwdriver, and sometimes a wrench. We want to fill your BFRB toolbox with lots of options so you can pick just the right one when you need it!

SEE, REFLECT, REDIRECT: NOTICING AND CHANGING BEHAVIORS

Sometimes, we do things without thinking—like biting our nails, picking at our skin, or pulling out hair. The key to stopping these habits is to **See, Reflect, and Redirect** what's happening!

- ★ See—Notice when your BFRB is happening.
- ★ Reflect—Think about your 5 W's and your SET up.
- ★ Redirect—Choose something else to do instead!

See: Paying Attention to Your Body

One way to get better at noticing habits is by practicing mindfulness. Mindfulness means paying close attention to what's happening right now—how your body feels, what you hear, and even how you're breathing. Here's a simple way to try it:

1. Sit comfortably and take a few deep breaths.
2. Close your eyes (if you want) and notice how the air feels as you breathe in and out.
3. Imagine a warm light moving slowly from your head to your toes.
4. As the light moves, pay attention to each part of your body—your forehead, your nose, your mouth, your neck, your body and arms, your hands, your legs, and your feet.
5. If you feel an itch or a tingle, just **see** it without doing anything.

By practicing this, you can get better at paying attention to your body and **seeing** when a BFRB is about to happen!

There are other ways to get really good at seeing your BFRB before or right as it starts. Here are some other ways to practice noticing your BFRB:

- ✓ Wear a special bracelet that vibrates, like the HabitAware Keen bracelet, if you move your hands a certain way, like touching your hair or face, when you do your BFRB. The little buzz helps you stop and reflect!

- ✓ Wear scented lotions or jingling bracelets that remind you when your hands are moving toward your BFRB spot.
- ✓ Click the button on a tally counter or write a check mark on a piece of paper each time you see your BFRB.

Reflect: Doing the Detective Work

Now that you can **see** your BFRB, it's time to **reflect**—why is it happening? Be a detective, find your clues, and write down what you discover.

- ✓ Use a simple notebook or the 5 W's chart to write down what you notice when you see the BFRB—the Who, What, When, Where, and Why your BFRB is S(ensations), E(motions), T(houghts) up.

Reflecting on your BFRB helps you understand it better, which makes it easier to change!

Redirect: Choosing Something Else to Do

Once you **see** your habit and **reflect** on why it happens, it's time to **redirect**—change what you do! Here we go—this chapter and the next chapter are jam-packed with tools to redirect your BFRB. So, let's get started.

TOOLS FOR MY 5 W'S

Who—As you go through life, you'll meet all kinds of people. Some of them will become important people in your journey—the ones you spend a lot of time with. It's awesome when these people are kind, supportive, and make you feel good. But sometimes, there are people who don't understand you or treat you unkindly, and that can make things harder. Think about the people you are around most of the time. Maybe they are your family, your friends, teachers, coaches, babysitters, or neighbors. How people treat you and how you treat others can have a big impact on your day and on your BFRB.

Who are the people in your life that you want to welcome on your passengers list?

....

....

....

....

....

....

What makes you want to have those people around you? How do they support you and make you feel loved?

....

....

....

....

....

....

Do you have people around you whom you don't really like? What do they do that makes you feel lonely, sad, unloved, or some other unwanted emotion?

....

....

....

....

....

....

What do the people around you do that feels helpful with your BFRB?

....

....

....

....

....

....

What do the people around you do that does not feel helpful with your BFRB?

....

....

....

....

....

....

Ideas for the Who's:

- ✓ Notice what you find to be helpful from other people and ask for help when you need it.
- ✓ Tell people when their behavior is not helpful and ask them to do something else instead.
- ✓ Do your best to distance yourself from the loud and unhelpful passengers in your life. Try not to give rides to people who don't deserve to be in your awesome race car!
- ✓ Understand that the people who love you may not always know how to help you. It is good to contact a professional who

understands BFRBs who can teach them how to be a good support person for you.

- ✓ It can be great to meet other kids and teens who also are built fancy and have a BFRB. You are not alone, and it can feel good to talk to people who have similar experiences.

Think about the questions you answered about relationships. Are there any ideas that could help you get more support from others? What is one small step you can try to do this week?

....

....

....

....

....

....

....

Think about the people you are around most of the time. Maybe they are your family, your friends, teachers, coaches, babysitters, or neighbors. How people treat you, and how you treat others, can have a big impact on your day and on your BFRB. There are some great tools that can help to improve your relationships with other people. One of the best "Who" tools is learning how to tell others how you feel in a way that helps you get the support you need. This can be tricky sometimes, especially with certain people, and it often takes practice. This tool is called *assertiveness*.

Sometimes people try to help, but what they do might not be very helpful. For example, imagine your sibling tries to stop you from biting your nails by grabbing your hand and telling your parents. This might feel like they're just trying to get you in trouble, and it could lead to a fight. That can make you feel stressed... and might even make you want to bite your nails more because you're feeling frustrated.

We can practice being assertive by talking to our siblings about how they can help in a different way. For example, you could say, "Hey Joey, it would really help me if you could use kind words when you notice me biting my nails, and maybe offer to play a game with me instead of grabbing my hand or telling on me. Can you help me with that?" Sometimes, we need a little help, and it's okay to talk to someone you trust about how to handle tough situations. Other times, we might need to avoid people who aren't being helpful or kind.

Have you ever noticed how good it feels to be around a good friend or spend time with your parent(s)? Or when you do something nice for someone important to you? It feels awesome to have those close relationships! These are the people who can be on your BFRB team! It's great to tell them how you feel and how they can be the most helpful. Sometimes, it takes a little thought, but think about how these people can support you. Keeping your BFRB a secret from the people who matter most can be stressful. You might feel embarrassed or worried they won't like you because of your picking, pulling, or biting. But when you learn more about your BFRB, it gets easier to talk to the people you trust. It feels amazing to have people who want to help!

Sometimes, kids like to join something called a "support group." It's a place where you can meet other awesome kids who are going through similar things! There are millions of people around the world with a BFRB, and some of them might even be reading this same book right now! How cool is that?

Can you think of someone in your life that causes you stress and stirs up your BFRB?

Who is someone that is easy and fun to be around?

....

....

....

....

....

What usually happens when you are around them?

....

....

....

....

....

How does your BFRB change when you are around them?

....

....

....

....

....

Is there anything you can say or do to make things better for you and your BFRB?

....

....

....

....

....

Is there anything others can say or do to make things better for you and your BFRB?

....

....

....

....

....

....

....

What—These are things around you that might make it easier to do your BFRB. It can help to remove or avoid these things, unless you really need them. For example, a lot of kids pick, pull, or bite when they're looking in the mirror. You could try taking down a mirror you don't need, putting up a reminder like a Post-It note, or using dry erase markers to write a note to not lean in too close. Some kids also use tweezers or other beauty tools when doing their BFRB. A fun trick is to freeze those tools in a block of ice, or ask a family member to keep them somewhere you can't get to.

Can you think of items that you use that make it easier to do your BFRB?

....

....

....

....

....

....

What can you do to not be around these items as much?

....

....

....

....

....

....

....

When—Throughout the day, kids have lots of routines. They get out of bed in the morning, go to the bathroom, brush their teeth, have breakfast, get ready for school, and more. Some kids might notice that their BFRB happens when they are feeling tired, brushing their teeth right before bed. Instead of brushing their teeth right before bed when they're too tired to notice or stop their BFRB, they could try brushing their teeth an hour earlier. This way, they're more awake and can say "No thanks!" to the BFRB.

When

Can you think of when you do your BFRB the most?

....

....

....

....

....

....

....

Is there another time or way that you could do this activity?

....

....

....

....

....

....

....

Where—It can be helpful to notice the places where your BFRB is most likely to happen. For example, if you tend to do your BFRB when you're alone in your bedroom reading, it might help to read in the living room with other people around. Some kids pick their nails, pull their hair, or bite their skin when they're watching a video and resting their arm on the chair's armrest. A good idea might be to sit somewhere else where you have to sit up straight, so you can't rest your arm in a way that makes it easier to do your BFRB.

Can you think of where you do your BFRB the most?

....

....

....

....

....

....

....

....

Is there a way for you to change your location to make it less likely for you to do your BFRB?

Why—You are really doing a great job being a detective! Look at all the great tips and tools you already learned by looking at the Who, What, When, and Where of your BFRB! Now, let's look at some of the Why's by looking at how your BFRB gets **SET** up, and gather tools so that you're ready for it!

Why—Satisfy My **S**enses
Why—Embrace My **E**motions
Why—Tame My **T**houghts

GATHER MY SET OF TOOLS

While you can't always prevent your BFRB from being SET up, you can gather a SET of tools so that you are ready for it when it happens. Being prepared is key to mastering your BFRB! Let's start with the S. What can you do when **Sensations** SET up your BFRB? You can explore fun and interesting ways to:

Satisfy My Senses

Build a Sensational Sensations Kit

Here's a fun activity: build your own sensational sensations kit—you might call this your "BFRB Box," "Fidget Fund," "Tool Tote," "Sensory Station," or some other name just for your creation. This is going to be a special place where you'll keep the things you'll use when your BFRB is SET up. You can use a small empty box, a plastic sand bucket, small wooden box, or some other container that you like. You can decorate it, too! Some kids like to draw pictures on their boxes or cut and paste photos on their boxes. It's up to you. Make it yours! Think of it as your treasure chest.

What might you call YOUR box?

....

....

....

....

....

....

Okay, let's talk about our senses. We have five of them:

1. Seeing
2. Hearing
3. Touching
4. Smelling
5. Tasting

   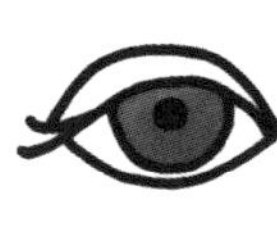 

Our senses help us understand the world around us. If you have a BFRB, some of the feelings you get from doing your BFRB might seem interesting or even feel good. That can make you want to do it more, even if you don't like what happens afterward. So, let's explore different sensations you might enjoy that you can try instead of your BFRB!

You can work with a grown-up to pick out fun sensory items for a special "BFRB box." (Shopping for sensory supplies can be super fun!) You can test things out in stores or look online for cool items to add to your box. Once your boxes are filled, keep them in the places where you usually do your BFRB so they're ready when you need them.

Here's an example of what a BFRB box might look like:

Seeing—Sometimes, what we see can make us want to do our BFRB. For example, Maya likes to look at her eyelashes and eyebrows in the mirror. When she notices a hair that looks out of place—like an eyelash pointing in a different direction—she feels the urge to pull it out.

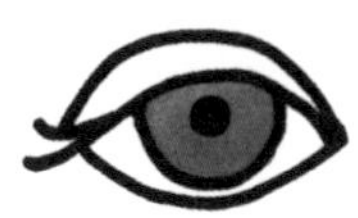

When Maya finds herself examining her eyebrows and eyelashes, what might she do instead?

You can also use **seeing sensation tools** to keep your eyes busy in a fun way! Here are some cool ideas:

- ✓ Watching YouTube videos
- ✓ Playing video games or apps
- ✓ Coloring, drawing, or painting
- ✓ Looking at pictures or photo albums
- ✓ Watching a lava lamp or fish tank
- ✓ Reading a book or comic
- ✓ Doing a puzzle or word search
- ✓ Playing with light-up or glow-in-the-dark toys
- ✓ Watching clouds, stars, or nature outside
- ✓ Using a kaleidoscope or looking at glitter jars
- ✓ Writing a poem or a story
- ✓ Making a craft
- ✓ Playing with gears
- ✓ Playing with a Rubik's Cube
- ✓ Playing with squeezy, popping toys

What seeing sensation tools might you like to use? What might you like to look at instead when what you see sets up your BFRB? Draw or write your ideas in the boxes below:

What are MY seeing sensation tools?		

Hearing—Sometimes, hearing sets up a BFRB. For example, Elliot likes the snapping sound he hears when he chews on his fingernails and toenails.

When Elliot finds himself wanting to bite on a nail to hear that snap, what might he do instead?

....

....

....

....

....

....

Sounds are hearing sensation tools. Here are some ideas for **hearing tools** to keep your ears busy:

- ✓ Listening to YouTube videos or podcasts
- ✓ Playing video games or fun apps with cool sounds
- ✓ Jamming out to your favorite music
- ✓ Talking or laughing with friends and family
- ✓ Trying a mindful listening meditation
- ✓ Playing with fidget toys that make sounds (like clicky buttons, rainmakers, or maracas)
- ✓ Popping bubble wrap (so satisfying!)
- ✓ Cracking sunflower seeds or crunchy snacks
- ✓ Snapping dry spaghetti noodles
- ✓ Listening to audiobooks or bedtime stories
- ✓ Tapping pencils or drumming fingers on a surface
- ✓ Blowing into a kazoo or harmonica
- ✓ Listening to nature sounds (like ocean waves, rain, or birds chirping)
- ✓ ASMR (tingly, calming sounds) videos or soundscapes
- ✓ Whispering a silly word over and over (try it—it's fun!)
- ✓ Playing with a white noise machine or sound app

What hearing sensation tools might you like to use? What might you like to listen to instead when what you hear sets up your BFRB? Draw or write your ideas in the boxes below:

What are MY hearing sensation tools?		

Touching—Sometimes, the way something feels can make you want to do your BFRB. For example, Maya notices little bumps on her skin or rough spots from a scab, and she starts picking at them without even thinking.

But what if Maya had a different way to keep her hands busy when she feels those textures? What could she do instead?

....

....

....

....

....

....

....

....

....

....

Sometimes, **touching sensation tools**—having different textures to feel—can help keep your hands busy and give you the sensations you like without doing your BFRB. Here are some cool touching sensation ideas to try:

- ✓ Bristly and stringy—Makeup brush, paint brush, loofah, body brush, mascara wand, toothbrush, string, dental floss, doll hair, burlap, Velcro, pipe cleaners
- ✓ Soft and fuzzy—String, dental floss, doll hair, fleece, microfiber cloth, silk ribbon, pom-poms, fuzzy socks, moss, feathers, velvet

- ✓ Smooth and hard—Beads, marbles, jewelry, polished stones, acorns, seashells, coins, smooth buttons, pinecones, stones, leaves, flower petals, bubble wrap, Calm Strips

- ✓ Sticky and peeling—Bubble wrap, dried glue to peel, wax strips, nail polish, sticky notes, silicone patches

- ✓ Squishy and stretchy—Stress ball, foam roller, slime, foam clay, gel bead packs, stretchy bracelets, Koosh ball, rubber bands, Thera-Band

- ✓ Hot and cold—Ice cube, warm bath, heat pack, cooling gel, frozen washcloth, icy drinks

- ✓ Movable and shapeable—Kinetic sand, Play-Doh, Silly Putty, clay, fidget putty, modeling beeswax, Tangle, paperclip, puzzle ring, origami, pen topper

- ✓ Soft and cuddly—Touching a family pet, stuffed animal, pillows, soft blankets

- ✓ Soothing and comforting—Lotion, aloe vera, facial mask, essential oil roller, cooling eye mask, Vicks VapoRub, astringent, cortisone cream, Lacri-Lube ointment, Aspercreme with Lidocaine, Icy Hot, eyebrow gel, weighted blanket

What touching sensation tools might you like to use? What might you like to touch instead when what you touch sets up your BFRB? Draw or write your ideas in the boxes below:

What are MY touching sensation tools?		

Smelling—Sometimes, certain smells can make someone want to do their BFRB. For example, Maya likes the way her hair smells after using shampoo, so she finds herself smelling the hairs she pulls.

When Maya notices this, what could she do instead? Maybe she could find other things that smell nice, like a scented lotion, a fun-smelling ChapStick, or a piece of fabric sprayed with her favorite scent. What other ideas can you think of?

....

....

....

....

....

....

Scents to smell are **smelling sensation tools**. Sometimes, certain smells can be really comforting or interesting! If you like using your sense of smell, here are some fun ideas to try instead of your BFRB:

- ✓ Scented lotions (Pick your favorite scent, like vanilla, strawberry, or lavender!)
- ✓ Bath salts or bubble baths (We can almost smell the relaxation just thinking about it!)
- ✓ Scented candles, oils, or incense (Be sure to ask a grown-up to help—they'll enjoy them too!)
- ✓ Perfumes and scented sprays (Spritz and smell!)
- ✓ Peel citrus fruit (Lemons, limes, and oranges can smell so nice!)
- ✓ Bake cookies (Ask a grown-up about this one, too! Okay, this one is also yummy to eat!)
- ✓ Scented markers, crayons, or stickers (They're fun to collect, too!)
- ✓ Fresh flowers or herbs
- ✓ Sachets or scented pouches

What smelling sensation tools might you like to use? What might you like to smell instead when what you smell sets up your BFRB? Draw or write your ideas in the boxes below:

What are MY smelling sensation tools?		

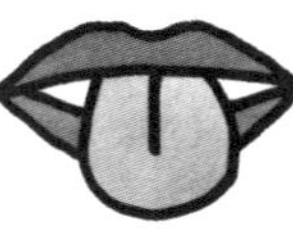

Tasting—Sometimes, the taste sensation sets up a BFRB. For example, Elliot chews on the nails that he bites. He finds the crunching sensation and the taste interesting.

When Elliot finds himself biting his nails, what might he do instead?

....

....

....

....

....

....

Sometimes, having something to chew, suck on, or taste can be a great way to keep your mouth busy instead of doing your BFRB. These are **tasting sensation tools**! Here are some fun tasting sensation ideas to try:

- ✓ Chewing seeds (sunflower, pumpkin, sesame, or poppy seeds)
- ✓ Crunching on dry spaghetti
- ✓ Mints or gum (peppermint, cinnamon, or bubblegum flavors!)
- ✓ Pulling apart and eating celery strands or string cheese
- ✓ Enjoying a crunchy snack (carrots, apples, pretzels, nuts, or popcorn)
- ✓ Chewy or gummy candy (like gummy bears or fruit chews)
- ✓ Sucking on hard candy (like lollipops, jawbreakers, or other long-lasting flavors)
- ✓ Having a hot or cold drink (like hot chocolate, tea, lemonade, or smoothies)
- ✓ Chewing on a toothpick, straw, or coffee stirrer
- ✓ Chewing chewable jewelry (like silicone necklaces or bracelets, sometimes called "chewelry")
- ✓ Using dental floss
- ✓ Tingly lip balm or flavored ChapStick (minty, fruity, or sweet!)
- ✓ Frozen fruit (like grapes, mango, strawberries, or blueberries)
- ✓ Crunching on ice chips or crushed ice
- ✓ Chewing on cinnamon sticks

What tasting sensation tools might you like to use? What might you like to taste instead when what you taste sets up your BFRB? Draw or write your ideas in the boxes below:

What are MY tasting sensation tools?		

Make a Treasure Hunt

Let's make a special calming container filled with glitter and little objects to find! This jar isn't just pretty—it's a fun way to focus on noticing your senses. You'll watch, shake, and explore the jar whenever your BFRB shows up or when you just need a break or want to focus.

What you'll need:

1. A clear plastic or glass jar with a tight lid (like a mason jar or sturdy water bottle)
2. Warm water
3. Clear glue or glitter glue
4. Fine glitter (your favorite colors!)
5. Small objects (like beads, buttons, tiny plastic animals, or sequins)
6. Food coloring (optional, for color)
7. A spoon or stick to stir
8. Super glue (to seal the lid—ask a grown-up to help)

Steps to make it:

1. **Fill the Jar with Warm Water:**
   Pour warm water into the jar until it's about three-quarters full. The warm water helps everything mix easily.

2. **Add Glue for a Swirly Effect:**
   Add clear glue or glitter glue to the jar (about 1/4 of the jar or more if you want things to move slower). The glue makes the glitter float and swirl.

3. **Sprinkle in Glitter:**
   Add a few spoonfuls of glitter. Mix different colors for a sparkly, magical look. This is what will catch your eye and make the jar fun to shake and watch.

4. **Add Tiny Objects to Find:**
   Drop in small objects like beads, sequins, buttons, or tiny plastic shapes. These will float and hide in the glittery mix. They'll make your jar into a sensory treasure hunt!

5. **Choose a Color (Optional):**
   Add a drop or two of food coloring if you want the water to have a tint. Stir gently and watch the color spread.

6. **Top Off with Water:**
   Fill the jar to the top, leaving just a little space so things can move around when you shake it.

7. **Stir the Magic Together:**
   Use a spoon or stick to mix everything. Watch how the glitter and objects move—What do you see? What do you hear when you tap the jar gently?

8. **Seal the Lid Tightly:**
   Ask a grown-up to use super glue to seal the lid shut. This keeps the water and glitter safely inside.

9. **Shake, Watch, and Explore:**
   Shake your jar and watch the glitter swirl like a tiny galaxy. Try finding the little objects as they float around. Can you count them? What colors do you see?

The sensory experience:

- **Seeing:** Shake it and watch the glitter settle. As you look for hidden objects, take deep breaths. Imagine your thoughts settling just like the glitter. Watch the glitter sparkle and the tiny objects twirl. Look closely to see how the colors and shapes change as they settle.
- **Hearing:** Listen closely—can you hear the water swishing inside?
- **Touching:** Hold the jar in your hands and feel its weight. Turn it upside down, shake it hard, or tilt it gently to see how things move.

Blockers

Did you know that roadblocks aren't just obstacles—they're one of the best ways to keep traffic flowing safely? Roadblocks help prevent accidents and keep everything moving smoothly. In the same way, you can create roadblocks to help stop your BFRB before it starts.

Are you ready to become a BFRB-blocking expert? Let's explore some smart ways to put roadblocks in place!

Some of the best tools for your BFRB toolbox are **roadblocks**—things that make it harder for your BFRB to happen. But what does "blocking" mean? It's when you place something in the way, just like a roadblock, to help steer yourself toward a different path. For example, Maya picks the skin on her hands and feet when watching TV, so she wears Band-Aids on her thumbs and pointer fingers during her favorite shows. Elliot bites his fingernails in the car, so he wears gloves when going for a ride.

There are lots of creative ways to make it harder to do a BFRB and block those urges! Here are some ideas you can try:

- ✓ Wear Vaseline on your eyelashes or eyebrows to make them slippery
- ✓ Try braiding your hair, wearing barrettes, or styling it in a style that makes hair harder to pull
- ✓ Wear rubber fingertips or finger cots to cover fingers used in doing the BFRB
- ✓ Use Band-Aids or liquid Band-Aids on your fingertips or to cover any scabs
- ✓ Keep your hair wet or use hair products to change the texture of your hair
- ✓ Cover areas you tend to pick or pull from with comfy clothing or nail stickers
- ✓ For head hair, try wearing a hoodie, headband, bandana, other head covering, or wig
- ✓ Try acrylic nails for a new, cool look

Can you think of other ideas for things that can block your BFRB? Draw or write the blockers you could use below:

What are MY blocker tools?		

Embrace My Emotions

We are moving on to the "E" to learn helpful and fun ways to *embrace your emotions* when feelings SET up your BFRB!

Noticing and Naming Emotions

The first emotion tool is all about noticing and naming what you're feeling! When you start to feel emotions that make you want to do your BFRB, go to page 63 in Chapter 3 and check out the emotion faces you colored in. Find the one that matches how you're feeling and say the name of that emotion, either in your head or out loud! If your feeling isn't on that page, don't worry—you can still figure it out! The more you practice, the better you'll get at understanding and naming your emotions.

TIBS

Have you ever felt so upset, angry, or anxious that your emotions felt like huge waves crashing over you? A lot of people with BFRBs feel the urge to do their BFRB when their emotions are really strong. The TIBS skills are special tools that can help you calm those big waves in ways that don't involve doing your BFRB. They're here to help you feel in control and find better ways to cope!

The TIBS skills are:

T—Temperature
I—Intense Exercise
B—Birthday Cake Breathing
S—Squeeze and Relax

Let's dive into these tools!

Temperature

Cold temperatures can help cool down those hot emotions!

Try:

- ★ Holding an ice cube in your hands and/or rubbing it on your face
- ★ Splashing cold water on your face
- ★ Taking a cool or cold shower
- ★ Putting an ice pack on your cheeks and eyes

Are there other temperature ideas you have? Write them here!

....

....

....

....

....

....

....

Intense Exercise

Big waves of emotion have a lot of energy, so you can use that energy to do something strong and powerful to help calm the waves down! Moving your body or doing something active can help you feel more in control and cool things off.

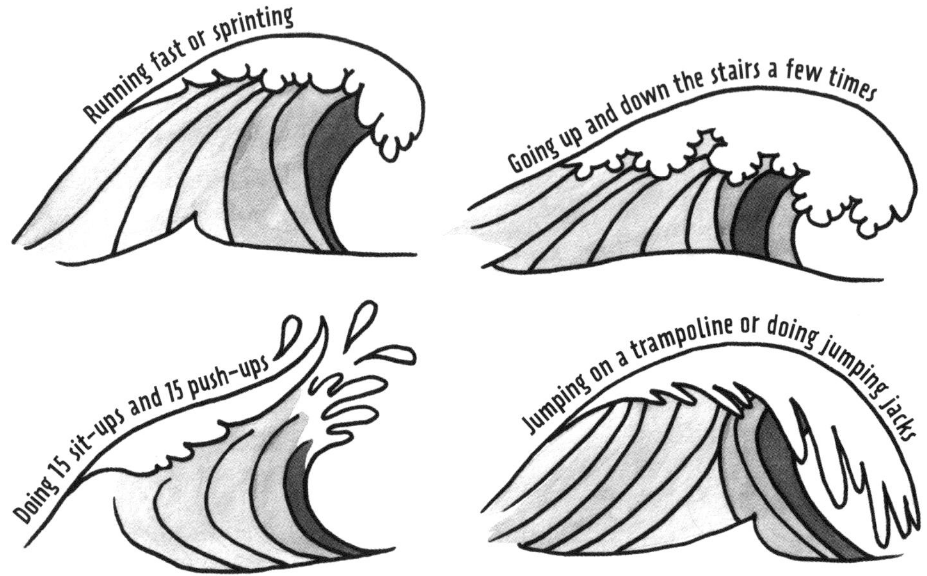

Try:

- Running fast or sprinting
- Going up and down the stairs a few times
- Doing 15 sit-ups and 15 push-ups
- Jumping on a trampoline or doing jumping jacks

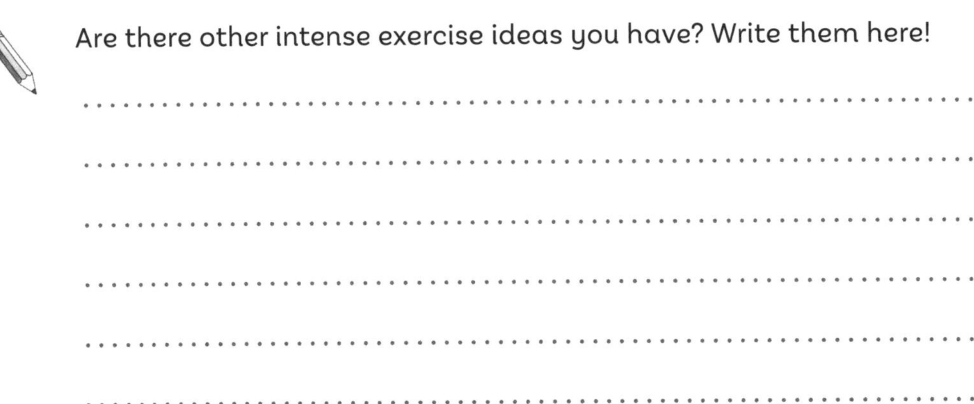

Are there other intense exercise ideas you have? Write them here!

Birthday Cake Breathing

When we feel anxious or upset, taking deep breaths can help calm our bodies down. Here's a fun way to try it!

Close your eyes and imagine it's your birthday, and there's a big chocolate birthday cake right in front of you. Slowly breathe in the yummy smell of the cake, and let your belly fill up with air like a birthday balloon. Breathe in for 1...2...3...4...5.

Now blow out the candles slowly, letting your balloon belly deflate as the air comes out. 1...2...3...4...5...6. Try doing this five times. The more you practice, the better you will get at calming your body down!

Squeeze and Relax

Many kids do their BFRB when they are feeling anxious or worried. When we are anxious, often our bodies become tense. Squeezing and relaxing our muscles is an emotion tool that can help you relax your body and feel less anxious. Here is how to do it!

1. Close your eyes and pretend you have a piece of candy in your mouth that you want to break into. Bite down hard with your jaw and hold it. Really clench your teeth. Feel all the muscles in your face and mouth working. Now, let go of your bite and let your jaw hang loose. Open your eyes—how do the muscles of your face feel?

2. Close your eyes again and imagine you have a lemon in each hand. You want to squeeze as much juice as possible out of those lemons. Squeeze your fists as tightly as you can. Feel your hands and arms get really tight. Now, let go of the lemons and notice how your hands feel after releasing the tension.

3. Now, let's pretend you're a cat and want to stretch your body out long and lean. Close your eyes and stretch your arms straight out high up above you—how high can you reach? Hold that stretch for a few moments. Then, release and allow your body to return to its comfortable position. Open your eyes—how do your arms feel now?

4. Imagine you're lying on the ground in the jungle. Close your eyes and picture the jungle around you. Uh oh, here comes a baby elephant! The baby elephant steps right onto your stomach. Keep your stomach muscles tight like a board to hold up that elephant. Hold it for a few moments. Whew! The elephant is walking away. You can let go and relax your stomach. Uh oh, here comes that baby elephant again! Tense your tummy muscles tight like a board and hold it, then relax. Open your eyes—how does your stomach feel now?

5. Here's your last challenge! Close your eyes and pretend you're splashing in the rain with your rain boots. You see a mud puddle. Push your feet down into the mud as hard as you can. Make your boots sink in. Keep pushing. Now, slowly bring your boots up out of the mud and relax your legs and feet. How do your legs and feet feel now?

Bringing Your Emotion to Life

This tool helps you imagine your feelings as something outside of you, like a cloud in the sky. By doing this, it's easier to accept your emotions and let them come and go, just like the weather.

Imagine your emotion is something you can hold in your hands, like an object. Picture it floating in front of you, where you can look at it and see it clearly. This can make your feelings feel less overwhelming and easier to handle! Imagine this emotion and see if you can answer these questions about it:

What shape and size is it? Describe it.

....

....

....

....

....

Is it a solid object or is it in another form, like a gas or a liquid?

Does the object have color? If it does, describe what it looks like.

Does it have texture? If so, describe that.

Is it moving? If so, how is it moving?

Is it making a sound? If so, what does it sound like?

....

....

....

....

....

Does it have a smell? If so, what does it smell like?

....

....

....

....

....

Can you imagine what it would feel like if you were to touch it? What would it feel like?

....

....

....

....

....

If you reach out to touch it, what does it do? Does it change or move in any way?

....

....

....

....

....

Are you ready to let the emotion back into your body, even if you don't want to feel it and don't like it? When you allow your feelings to be there instead of trying to push them away, it helps you do things you enjoy, like talking to your friends or playing a game. This way, you're not stuck doing things you don't want to do, like yelling at others or doing your BFRB. Letting your feelings be there can help you feel more in control and focus on what matters to you!

How do you feel now? Do you notice any difference between how you feel now and how you felt when you were first noticing this emotion?

Feeling Flippers

When you're feeling an emotion that makes you want to do your BFRB, you can "flip" that feeling into the opposite one! For example, if you tend to do your BFRB when you're bored, try making a list of fun things to do, like writing a story, playing a game, or jumping on the trampoline. If you do your BFRB when you're feeling sad, do something that makes you happy, like baking cookies with a parent, drawing a picture, or doing something nice for someone. Flipping your feelings can help you feel better and do something fun instead!

Here is a list of difficult feelings that could make you do your BFRB and examples of Feeling Flippers. Write your own ideas in the blank spaces!

Feeling Flippers	
Bored	**Stressed/Anxious**
✓ Write a story comic strip, or poem ✓ Play or learn an instrument, like guitar ✓ Go on a bike ride ✓ Jump on a trampoline ✓ Learn a skill like a handstand or backbend ✓ Make bracelets ✓ Paint or draw ✓ .... ✓ .... ✓ .... ✓	✓ Take a bath (add a glowstick, bubbles, or bath salts for colored fun!) ✓ Listen to your favorite music ✓ Read a book ✓ Coloring ✓ Take a walk and focus on sights, smells, and sounds ✓ Make slime or play with playdough ✓ .... ✓ .... ✓ .... ✓ ....
Sad	**Angry**
✓ Practice a sport like shooting basketballs or kicking a soccer ball or playing catch ✓ Talk to a family member or friend ✓ Watch funny videos ✓ Play with a pet ✓ Write a list of things you are grateful for ✓ .... ✓ .... ✓ .... ✓ .... ✓	✓ Do something nice for someone like make them a card or bring them a treat or say something nice to them ✓ Watch your favorite show or a new movie you have been wanting to watch ✓ Play a favorite game like a board game or card game or video game ✓ Do a puzzle or build with Legos ✓ Dance to upbeat, fun music ✓ .... ✓ .... ✓ .... ✓ ....
Other Emotion: ____________	**Other Emotion: ____________**
✓ .... ✓ .... ✓ .... ✓ .... ✓	✓ .... ✓ .... ✓ .... ✓ .... ✓ ....

In the picture on pages 142 and 143, Maya and Elliot are enjoying a beautiful day outdoors. Use your crayons, markers, or colored pencils to bring the scene to life—and think about what they might be experiencing with each of their senses!

Sound—What might they be hearing? Color in the chirping birds, bleating sheep and lambs, rushing waterfall, babbling brook, crashing waves, and Elliot munching on cake.

Smell—Imagine all the wonderful smells around them! Color the blossoming tree, blooming flowers, delicious chocolate cake, juicy fruit, fresh lemonade, and clean, fresh air.

Taste—Yum! Color the tasty treats Maya and Elliot can enjoy: a crisp apple, sweet pear, tangy tangerine, cool lemonade, and yummy cake.

Touch—What can they feel? Color the warm sun on their faces, the soft grass under their feet, the splashy waterfall, the squishy mud beneath Maya's feet, and the rough tree bark.

Sight—What do they see? Color the bright rainbow, shining sun, fluffy clouds, rolling hills, and anything else you find in the picture!

Let your imagination guide you—and don't forget to use all your senses as you color!

When your emotions are strong, and you feel a strong urge to do your BFRB, you can practice *Soothing with Your Five Senses* to help you tame those emotions!

See: Find soothing things to look at, like:

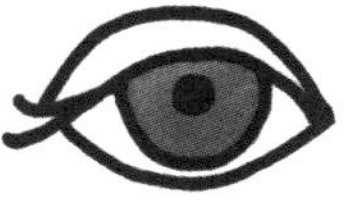

- ✓ your pet
- ✓ favorite photos
- ✓ a pretty sky, or a rainbow
- ✓ or just find five things you can spot around you!

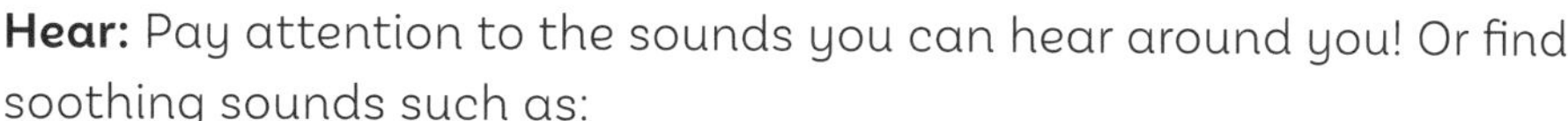

Hear: Pay attention to the sounds you can hear around you! Or find soothing sounds such as:

- ✓ soothing music
- ✓ playing an instrument
- ✓ birds chirping
- ✓ a trickling stream, faucet, or waterfall.

Touch: Find a few soothing things you can touch, like:

- ✓ a soft blanket
- ✓ running water
- ✓ your pet's fur
- ✓ blades of grass.

Smell: Notice the scents you smell. Find soothing scents like:

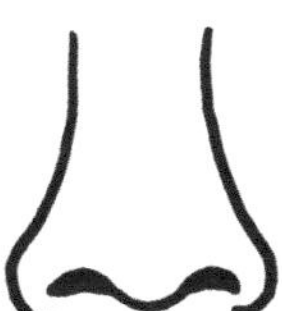

- ✓ a candle, flowers, or herbs
- ✓ fresh fruit
- ✓ fresh outdoor smells
- ✓ fresh baked goodies!

Taste: Taste something yummy and savor the flavor! Try some of these:

- ✓ chocolate
- ✓ mints
- ✓ a yummy warm drink
- ✓ a favorite snack.

Color the senses!

Can you think of any other five senses ideas? Write them below:

See	Hear	Touch	Smell	Taste

Riding the Wave

Imagine you're a surfer riding a big wave along the shore. You catch the wave as it rises, ride it as it peaks, and stay on your surfboard until it falls. Emotions and urges to pick or pull are like those waves. They can get bigger and stronger, but eventually, they'll calm down and fall. Emotions and urges come and go, just like waves, even if you don't give in or try to fight them. Waves can feel powerful, but if you get on your surfboard and ride the wave, it will eventually pass. The surfboard helps you stay steady, in control, and moving in the direction you want!

Let's try it! When you have a strong emotion or urge, rate how strong your emotion or urge is from 1 to 10.

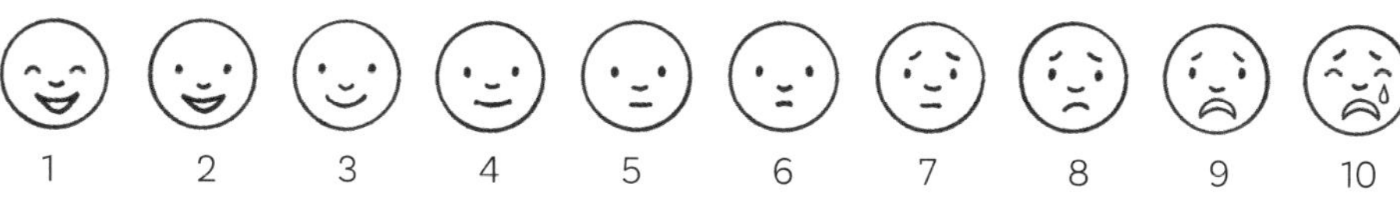

The awesome thing about surfing is that you can learn to surf those waves of emotion, and with practice, you can get good at it! Close your eyes and picture yourself on a surfboard, watching the wave rise up. Take slow, deep breaths and let the emotion or urge be there without trying to get rid of it or push it away. Instead of judging yourself, be kind to yourself for having that feeling. Feelings are okay to have, no matter what they are. Just like surfing, the more you practice, the better you'll get at handling your emotions!

What is going on in your body as you ride the wave?

Tell yourself that this feeling will pass, and that you can stay on the board and ride that wave until it calms down. You can use any of your emotion tools you have learned so far to help you stay on that board and ride that wave!

How strong was your emotion or urge when it peaked?

1 2 3 4 5 6 7 8 9 10

How long did the emotion or urge last?

How strong was your emotion or urge toward the end of your surfing?

....

....

....

....

....

How well did you do riding that wave?

....

....

....

....

....

What helped you ride the wave?

....

....

....

....

....

Tame My THOUGHTS

Now, let's talk about the "T" in SET—it's all about being more aware of your **thoughts** and learning how to respond differently to the ones that make you want to do your BFRB! Think of your thoughts like the digital controls on a fancy car. It's helpful most of the time, but sometimes it gives us an error message or tries to take us the wrong way. Don't worry though—there are lots of great ways to handle those tricky thoughts, and we can't wait to share our favorite thought-hacking tools with you!

Our thoughts are very important because they affect how we feel and what we do. For example, if you think "I want to try some of these cool skills in the workbook," you might feel excited and hopeful. That can make you want to try out the new tools you're learning! Thoughts are really powerful, so it's good to notice how they affect your BFRB. Many kids say they think, "I can't stop my BFRB." Have you ever noticed this thought? How does it make you feel? If you feel sad or frustrated, you might feel the urge to pick, pull, or bite. This is when we can get stuck in a loop of unhelpful thoughts, big emotions, and wanting to do our BFRB. But—we can break out of that loop! Let's figure out what patterns you notice in your thoughts and BFRB, so you can start to feel more in control.

Thought →	→ Emotion(s) →	→ Behavior(s)
"I can't stop this."	Frustrated, sad, ashamed	Pull, pick, hide in my room

Let's start by talking about how to reprogram those unhelpful "error" messages in your mind. Think of them like the warning lights on a car dashboard. When something's not quite right—like low tire pressure or an engine issue—the dashboard lights up to let you know. In the same way, these mental "error messages" are signals that a thought might be off or unhelpful. If we ignore them, they can lead to uncomfortable feelings and trigger your BFRB. But just like a driver can check the issue and reset the warning, you can learn to catch those thought errors and shift them. It's a great skill, and it just takes a few simple steps!

First, we need to spot the unhelpful thought. These thoughts pop up on their own, and you don't choose to have them. They can make you feel different emotions and sometimes lead to your BFRB. Here are some examples of those "pop-up error message" thoughts that might trigger your BFRB:

Perfectionism—A thought that everything has to be or feel just right. ("I can't have any rough spots on my skin." "My eyelashes all need to be the same length.")

Permissiveness—Giving yourself the "okay" to do something that doesn't match your goals or beliefs. ("I am gonna start working on this tomorrow." "I'll only bite my nails for one minute." "I'll just pull this one wild hair.")

Can'ting—Telling yourself that you cannot do something even though it may be possible. ("I can't stop picking my skin." "I can't control this while I am doing homework.")

Unrealistic Expectations—Having really big goals for yourself that most people cannot reach. ("As soon as I start working on this, I will never do my BFRB again." "I will never again pick my scabs.")

Mind Reading—Thinking that we know what other people are thinking, even though we really don't know. ("They think I'm weird because I don't have eyebrows." "They don't want to be my friend.")

Fortune Telling—These thoughts make us feel like we have a magic crystal ball and can see into the future. ("I'm not going to be able to go to the beach this summer because of my picking." "No one will want to date me when I grow up.")

Catastrophizing—These are the super dramatic thoughts that tend to be pretty extreme. ("If someone at school sees my bald spot, everyone will talk about me and I will lose my friends. I will need to stay home and will not be able to ever go to school.")

Negative Filtering—This happens when we ignore the stuff we like about ourselves and only focus on the stuff we don't like. ("I look bad today; my eyelashes are almost completely gone." "These scars on my arm make me look ugly.")

What If?—Asking yourself "what if?" questions about things you're not sure about yet. ("What if someone notices my hair?" "What if my hat comes off?")

Overgeneralization—Thinking that something that happened recently will keep happening forever. ("I pulled/picked/bit so much today, I will always have my BFRB." "I have a new bald spot, I will never be able to control this behavior.")

Emotional Reasoning—This is the idea that just because we feel something, it must be true. ("I feel embarrassed and everyone is looking at me because of my BFRB." "These urges are making me do it.")

Should Statements—The thought that your experience has to be the same as everyone else's. When you have "should thoughts," you might feel guilty, frustrated, or angry. ("I shouldn't have this problem." "I should be able to just stop. My hair should look like other kids' in my class.")

All or Nothing—Seeing a situation as either all one way or the complete opposite with no in between. We sometimes call this black and white thinking because it's like seeing this as all black or all white, with no shades of gray. ("I already picked/pulled today, so I am a total failure." "I bit off one nail, so I need to bite off the rest.")

What are the error messages that pop up on your dashboard?

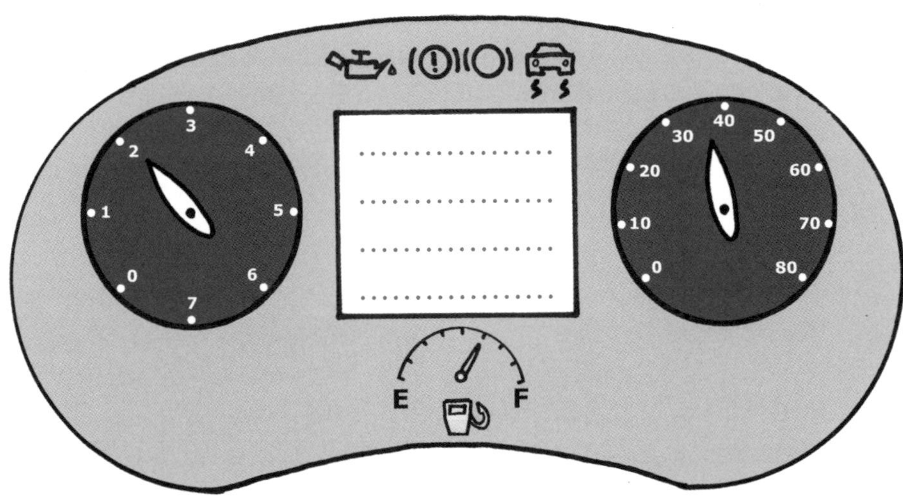

Now let's try to change those error messages so that they say something more helpful.

Error Message Thought	More Helpful Thought
Everyone is noticing my missing lashes and they think I am weird.	People may or may not notice, and lots of people pull their hair. I am a cool kid with or without eyelashes.

An easy way to remember this skill is to think, I CAN develop helpful, healthy self talk.

C—Catch the error message thought and notice how it makes you feel and want to act.
A—Ask yourself if this is a helpful or unhelpful message.
N—Name a more helpful thought that leads to more helpful emotions and actions.

Let's try it!

Changing the Error Message

Error Message Thought	How does this make me feel and behave?	Is this thought helpful or unhelpful?	What kind of error message is it?	What is a more helpful thought?	How does that new thought make me feel and behave?	Is this thought helpful or unhelpful?
I can't stop biting and picking my skin.	Sad, guilty; I go to my bathroom and pick.	Unhelpful	Can'ting	I am learning new ways to give my body what it needs. With practice, I can pick less.	Feeling better, more hopeful. I will try to use my new tools instead of going to the bathroom to pick.	Helpful

Awesome job! This is a great skill to help change those unhelpful error messages. Sometimes, even though we try really hard to replace them, they keep popping up—and that can be super annoying! But guess what? We don't have to believe everything we think. It's true! Sometimes, all we need to do is practice ignoring those "junk" thoughts. Let them be there, but try not to react to them.

Imagine you're a bus driver. And, there are lots of noisy passengers on the bus. Some of them are troublemakers who say unkind things that make you question where you're going. Others might try to help, but they're not giving the best advice. Some passengers are kind and encouraging. And guess what? Your BFRB Beast is on the bus too—because it's always with you. They might try to distract you or convince you to take a detour, especially when things get stressful. But if you are the driver and you listened to every single passenger—or stopped to argue with the loud or bossy ones—you'd never get anywhere! A smart bus driver focuses on where they want to go and learns to say "Thanks, but no thanks" to the unhelpful passengers... even the BFRB Beast. You're still the one driving the bus.

What kind of passengers show up on your bus?

Instead of trying to argue with those passengers or trying to push them out, do you think you could let them stay there without letting them take over the ride? Can you focus on the road ahead and where you want to go even if they get a little rowdy from time

to time? What does that look like for you? Try drawing a picture of where you want to go and what your passengers look like. How do these passengers affect your BFRB?

Getting Playful with Your Thoughts

Another cool way to handle unhelpful thoughts is to learn how to play with them! Instead of just believing them, try stepping back and seeing what they sound like. It's like turning your thoughts into something you can experiment with! Ready for a fun experiment? Let's give it a try!

Think about a bossy thought that you have where your mind is unkind to yourself.

I am ....

Now really sit with that thought and repeat it for 30 seconds. How does that feel?

Let's add a little something to the beginning of that same thought...

I am having the thought that I am ....

Let's back up even a bit more from the thought by adding this...

I notice that I am having the thought that I am ....

Did you notice how your feelings changed when you took a step back from the thought? With practice, the thought starts to lose its power and doesn't make you feel as strongly. It gets easier to keep some distance from it!

You can also play with error message thoughts by making them sound silly. There are lots of fun apps on smartphones (like Memoji, SnapChat, Funny Face Camera, Crazy Helium Funny Face Voice, Funny Face Masks, and many others) that allow you to change how you sound or look in videos. One cool trick is to record some of your unhelpful thoughts in a silly way! With your parent's permission, try recording yourself saying these thoughts in a funny chipmunk voice or make yourself look like a bunny rabbit.

What did you notice? It's usually a lot easier to laugh at those error message thoughts when they sound like a cartoon bunny! You can also pretend to be a dramatic actor and say these thoughts in an over-the-top way, like you're auditioning for a movie! Give your actor a fun name or even make it into a short film. If you're feeling really silly, you could turn it into a musical!

When you learn how to challenge, not overreact, and back up from unhelpful thoughts, it gives you more brain room and energy to focus on the positive stuff that helps you move in the direction you want to go.

Chapter 6

Rewarding Myself

"Just Like Me"

By Doug Schwarz, Photographer

My name is Doug and when I was a little boy around the age of seven, for what seemed like no reason at all, I started pulling out my hair. Sometimes one hair at a time, sometimes several! As bizarre as it seemed, I liked it! But bald patches started appearing, so my mom started getting me short haircuts to help me not pull. I felt so different, I felt weird! I never told any of the other kids at school, but one day in the 4th grade I had a friend over and I decided to tell him my secret. It felt so good to tell someone else what was going on with me, but the next day when I went to school, he had told the whole class! I was so embarrassed! I never talked to anybody about my secret ever again.

A couple of years went by, and my mom told me about a camp where I could meet other people who had the same strange thing as me! I was very unsure, but my mom made me go anyway, and I am so glad she did. We flew to San Francisco and took a bus full of people just like me to the redwood forests! We arrived at the camp, and I wanted to go home right away. But after a couple hours I started talking to some of the other kids, and the last thing I wanted to do was go home. I had the best time and no longer felt weird or strange or different. How could I after learning about how so many people do what I do but just don't talk about it!

Over the years I have made so many friends who pull their hair, pick their skin, chew their nails; many are my closest friends all thanks to these camps, also called retreats! I have gone to 15 retreats so far, and now that I'm an adult my friends and I are the ones putting them on! We actually are now hosting them on my farm in Oklahoma, where people can not only get together and meet up, go to classes and learn, but also enjoy hanging out with lots of animals like donkeys, goats, sheep, and pigs!

Turns out this weird, strange, crazy thing that made me feel so different was the best thing to ever happen to me!

Doug

Everyone deserves a reward for working hard, and working on your BFRB is definitely hard work! This chapter is all about how rewards can help you manage your BFRB even better.

STEP 1: WHAT WILL YOU GET REWARDS FOR?

The best way to use rewards is to celebrate when you use the tools you learned in this workbook—not just for avoiding your BFRB.

On the reward chart on page 161, write down the strategies you want to try or are already using, along with when you'll use them. For example, you could write, "Wear Band-Aids on my thumb and finger when I get home from school." You can check out an example of a completed reward chart on page 160 to get some ideas!

STEP 2: CHOOSE YOUR REWARDS!

What do you want to earn for practicing your strategies? With a parent or adult, decide on some rewards that you'll work toward for practicing your strategies (make sure your parent approves of them too!). Rewards can be things you can buy, or they can be special activities like picking the movie for movie night, staying up a little later, choosing the restaurant for a family dinner, or doing something fun with your parent(s) like going to the movies or baking cookies!

Write your reward list on page 161. You can see an example of a completed list on page 160. With a parent, decide how many points each reward is worth. You'll earn one point for every strategy you use.

STEP 3: TRACKING YOUR STRATEGIES!

Now, decide with a parent how you'll use your reward chart. You'll need a chart for each week. You can make copies of the chart to hang up around the house, laminate one to reuse each week, or even buy a reward chart online! Decide how you want to mark off your strategies—maybe with fun stickers, a star, a checkmark, or something else that feels exciting!

Instead of using a reward chart, you can try a fun jar! You can even decorate the jar to make it your own! Every time you use a strategy, add a pom-pom or poker chip to the jar. Once you've earned enough, you can trade your pom-poms or poker chips with a parent for a cool reward!

STEP 4: TURNING IN POINTS FOR REWARDS!

Now, decide with a parent when you'll turn in your points (or your pom-poms or poker chips!) for rewards. Some families let you turn them in at the end of the week for prizes, while others let you do it every night. If you have points left over after you get your reward, be sure to save them for next week!

Sometimes, a strategy might stop feeling fun because it gets boring or you just get tired of it. If that happens, you can swap it out for a new one from your list! Also, if you think of any new rewards you'd like to earn, add them to your list (just make sure your adult approves!).

We are excited for you to earn rewards for your hard work with your BFRB!! As you keep using your strategies to help you do your BFRB less, you will find the urge to pick or pull becomes weaker and weaker and you may not need to use your strategies as much!

STRATEGIES	M	T	W	Th	F	Sa	Su
Wearing Band-Aids when I come home from school	☆	☆	☆		☆		
Use a fidget (squish ball or spinner ring) at school		☆		☆			☆
Use castor oil in hair in the morning	☆		☆			☆	☆
Use muscle relaxation and coping thoughts when anxious	☆			☆	☆		
Go to sleep by 9pm!		☆		☆		☆	
Use Play-Dough while doing homework	☆			☆		☆	☆

Reward	Points
Get ice cream at favorite spot	5
Movie night	5
Get prize at 5 Below	10
Get to stay up an hour later	10
Go to race car track	10
Baking cookies with Mom	10
New video game	15
Amusement park trip	50

.... 's Rewards Chart

STRATEGIES	M	T	W	Th	F	Sa	Su

Reward	Points

Part III

GO

Chapter 7

Free to Be Me

"Just Like Me"

By Christy Garner, DC, Healthcare Practitioner, Advocate

Growing up in Minnesota, I was a bright, quirky kid who seemed to do well at everything I touched. My family often teased me that everything I did turned to gold—piano, school, sports—it all came naturally to me. But looking back, I now realize that my desire to do well was fueled by something deeper: a secret I was desperately trying to hide.

I repetitively pulled my hair, picked my skin, and bit my nails and cheeks. I didn't know anyone else who did these things, so I did everything I could to cover them up. I parted my hair in creative ways to hide the bald spots (notice my stylish Princess Leia buns in my photo! ha ha!). I wore long pants and sleeves to cover my scars. I told everyone that I kept my nails super short because of sports. The truth was, I was trying to keep everyone focused on my accomplishments so they wouldn't notice how much I was struggling inside.

The first time I learned that my behaviors had a name was in a class in college. The professor put up a photo of a woman with trichotillomania and explained that it was a medical condition where individuals pulled out their hair. I remember sitting there, surprised—this was real. This had a name. Quietly, I rubbed the bald spot above my ear and promised myself I would learn more.

Fast forward to today: I work with many gifted people with neurological differences such as ADHD, autism, dyslexia, and more. Many of them also have body-focused repetitive behaviors. Through my work, I've realized that these behaviors aren't something to be ashamed of. They are simply a strategy—a creative way that many of us manage our sensitive nervous systems in a world that wasn't necessarily built for our sensitivity. They are a cue that our bodies need something.

Some of my favorite people share this same sensitivity. Looking back, I wish I could give my younger self a hug and tell her she will find people just like her. That there's nothing to be ashamed of. That she will have a wonderful life full of love and success. And that these behaviors, while once a source of shame, were actually the things that gave me a special purpose in life.

Today, I am thankful for that journey. Because in understanding myself, I have been able to help others. And that, I believe, is the greatest success of all.

Christy

NAVIGATING BUMPS IN THE ROAD

You have collected so many tools for your toolbox to help you with your BFRB! When you practice using your tools again and again (and reward yourself for all of your hard work!), you may find that your BFRB Beast is smaller, or friendlier, or easier to get along with, or maybe he disappears for a while! Even with your BFRB Beast in tow, you can take charge of the wheel of your car on your life's journey, and choose where you want to go without your BFRB getting in the way!

The journey will not always be smooth and straight, though! There will be bumps in the road and curves and turns. Your BFRB Beast may come back if he left, or he may get louder at times. That's normal! Let's help you prepare for those bumps and curves!

BFRBs can show up again when there are changes in your life (good or bad or in-between!). Can you think of any changes coming up in your life? For example, starting a new school year, a new baby in the family, or starting a new sport. Write some upcoming changes below:

....

....

....

....

....

....

....

Stress can also make your BFRB grow. Can you think of any stressors or other triggers that may make your BFRB Beast grow louder in the future? For example, stressors could be getting a bad grade, getting in a fight with a friend, or having a big sports competition coming up. These may be the same triggers you identified when we learned about your BFRB. Write some stressors or triggers to watch out for below.

....

....

....

....

....

....

Let's talk about how to navigate those bumps in the road to get back on track! When there are bumps in the road, and your BFRB Beast gets a little louder, no need to worry! You did not lose all of your progress, so watch out for those "error messages" such as **All or Nothing Thinking** or **Catastrophizing**.

Overreacting to a bump in the road can steer you off course, so use your tools to tame those thoughts and help yourself stay on the road!

Another thing to look out for that can take you off course is to underreact to the bumps and curves and ignore your BFRB Beast getting louder and trying to get control of the wheel. You might notice you're doing your BFRB more, and have **Permissiveness** thoughts like:

The risky thing about this way of reacting is that your BFRB can become very big and strong again quickly, and then it may be much harder to manage, and you may steer off course!

Making a plan for bumps in the road can help you navigate those bumps with skill, and avoid veering off the road on either side! Whenever you find yourself doing your BFRB more, come back to your roadmap to help you use the skills in this book and get back on course.

ROADMAP FOR NAVIGATING BUMPS IN THE ROAD

Step One: If you notice your BFRB Beast is getting stronger again, take a look again at your Who, What, When, Where, and Why triggers. Are they the same as when you first filled out this workbook?

Step Two: First, check in on how you are taking care of that race car body of yours. Are you getting enough sleep, eating well and eating enough, and getting enough exercise and play? If not, work on taking care of yourself first!

Step Three: If you have been taking care of your body and your brain, and your BFRB is still bothering you, your next step is to start using some of your tools again. Which are the tools you would try first?

Step Four: If your BFRB has not been tamed with those tools after a few weeks, which other tools would you like to add?

Step Five: It is normal for your BFRB Beast to come and go in your life, getting louder and bigger at times, and other times quieter or weaker. If you are having trouble managing your BFRB by yourself or with your parents' or grown-ups' help, there are special therapists who help kids with their BFRBs. Talk to your parent(s) if you would like to get help from a therapist who knows all about BFRBs!

BECOMING FRIENDS WITH YOUR BFRB BEAST!

You've met your BFRB Beast and learned its tricks—but what if, instead of always fighting it, you got to know it a little better? What if you and your beast could be *friends*?

Sometimes, trying to get rid of a BFRB completely can feel really hard. But what if, instead of being mean to yourself about it, you showed yourself kindness? You and your beast are in this together, and that means you can still have fun, even when it's around!

If you and your BFRB Beast could have a fun day together, what would you do? Maybe you'd:

- ✓ Play your favorite video game together
- ✓ Draw or paint side by side
- ✓ Shoot hoops or kick a soccer ball around
- ✓ Read a book together
- ✓ Dance to your favorite music

What else might you do together?

....

....

....

....

....

....

....

....

Your beast doesn't have to be scary—it can be silly, playful, or even helpful!

Now, grab your markers, crayons, or colored pencils. You might even grab some stickers, googly eyes, or anything fun to decorate your beast and draw a picture of you and your beast doing something you love. Maybe your beast looks different when it's having fun—maybe it's smaller, or it's smiling instead of looking sneaky. Maybe it even cheers you on!

What activity did you and your beast do together?

....

....

....

....

How did your beast act when you played together?

....

....

....

....

....

How did *you* feel while having fun, even with your beast around?

....

....

....

....

....

If your beast could talk, what would it say to you when you're having fun?

....

....

....

....

....

Even if your BFRB is sometimes frustrating, it's part of your journey. You don't have to be mad at it all the time. The next time you feel bad about it, remember this drawing. You can still have fun, do cool things, and be *awesome*—even if your BFRB Beast is along for the ride.

Having a BFRB doesn't mean you can't have fun, enjoy life, or be *yourself*. You are *so much more* than your BFRB! It's just one small part of you—like your favorite color, the way you laugh, or the things that make you happy.

You don't have to wait until your BFRB is completely gone to do the things you love. You can play, create, explore, and be awesome *right now*, just the way you are!

So, go ahead—draw yourself and your BFRB Beast playing together, having fun, and enjoying life. Redefine who your beast is and how you get along with each other. Maybe your beast is there to remind you to:

Be aware of your triggers

Explore your toolbox tools

Accept all your sensations, emotions, and thoughts and ride those waves

Show kindness to your body and mind

Turn toward what matters most to you and be the person you want to be

Say it with us—"I'm free to be me with a BFRB!"

FTB ME